CITY OF NEW YORK

DEPARTMENT OF BRIDGES

Contracts with Railroad Companies

NEW YORK AND BROOKLYN BRIDGE

AND

WILLIAMSBURGH BRIDGE

PROPERTY OF
University of Michigan Libraries
1817
ARTES SCIENTIA VERITAS

CITY OF NEW YORK
DEPARTMENT OF BRIDGES

Contracts
with
Railroad Companies

New York & Brooklyn Bridge

AND

Williamsburgh Bridge

Transportation
Library

TG
25
.N5
A42
1906

1639-06

INDEX.

NEW YORK AND BROOKLYN BRIDGE.

	PAGE
Agreement, The Kings County Elevated Railway Company—Station Connection	5
Agreement, The Brooklyn City & Newtown Railroad Company—Washington Street Siding	11
Agreement, The Nassau Electric Railroad Company—Washington Street Siding	15
Agreement, The Brooklyn Heights Railroad Company (Trolley)	19
Agreement, Associated Trolley Companies—Relative to operation over New York and Brooklyn Bridge	37
Agreement (Original), Brooklyn Elevated Railroad Company	51
Agreement (Original), The Kings County Elevated Railway Company	65
Agreements (modified), Brooklyn Elevated Railroad Company and The Kings County Elevated Railway Company	79

WILLIAMSBURGH BRIDGE.

Agreements, The Brooklyn Heights Railroad Company, New York City Railway Company, The Coney Island & Brooklyn Railroad Company, Bridge Operating Company for operation of Surface Cars	100

AGREEMENT.

THE KINGS COUNTY ELEVATED RAILWAY COMPANY.

STATION CONNECTION.

THIS AGREEMENT, made this eighth day of November, in the year eighteen hundred and ninety-four, between THE TRUSTEES OF THE NEW YORK and BROOKLYN BRIDGE (hereinafter called "THE TRUSTEES") of the first part and THE KINGS COUNTY ELEVATED RAILWAY COMPANY (hereinafter called "THE COMPANY") of the second part, WITNESSETH:

That the parties in consideration of the premises, the mutual agreements herein contained and of One Dollar paid by each to the other, the receipt whereof is hereby acknowledged, mutually agree as follows:

First—The Trustees agree to construct and maintain the elevated passenger terminal platform and connecting stairways, within and over the property of the Trustees between Sands and High streets according to the plan deposited in the office of the Trustees marked "New Brooklyn station, 3d story plan, Drawing 4102, December 2, 1892."

Second—The Trustees hereby lease for the term of ten years from the completion of said platform and stairways to the Company and its successors, the right to have passengers seeking and leaving the railroad of the Company, and its officers and servants enter upon and pass over the portion of the said elevated passenger terminal platforms and stairways which are within the red lines upon the diagram hereto annexed. "The Trustees" agrees that it will during that term heat and light the premises and keep them in repair.

"The Company" agrees that it will, during said period, pay to "The Trustees" as an annual rent the sum of Four Hundred Dollars ($400) in equal quarterly installments commencing from the time when the premises shall be completed.

AND IT IS AGREED that if any payment shall remain due and unpaid thirty days after the same becomes due and payable, or if default shall be made in any of the covenants herein contained, then it shall be lawful for "The Trustees" to re-enter the premises and to remove all persons and all structures therefrom, and also all structures and connections of said railroad company over or upon the plaza or other bridge lands, and the expense of such removal shall be borne by the latter.

"The Company" covenants that it will not at any time during the continuance of this lease, either hinder or obstruct "The Trustees" from making such changes in the station, platform, tracks, etc., as "The Trustees" may desire, provided, however, that no change shall be made which shall substantially alter the character of the premises hereby leased or substantially affect its use by "The Company," without its consent, and all changes shall be at the expense of said "The Trustees."

IT IS MUTUALLY UNDERSTOOD AND AGREED that "The Company" shall care for all persons leaving its railroad, except employees of "The Trustees," until they enter upon the Bridge platform and leave the stairway leading thereto, and leaving the Bridge railroad and seeking "The Company's" elevated railroad from the time they first enter upon the stairway leading from the Bridge platform to the elevated railroad platform, and to this end "The Company" shall have the police and care of everything above the level of the Bridge platform, and "The Company" covenants that it will indemnify and save harmless "The Trustees" from all liability to all persons, except as aforesaid, leaving or seeking its elevated railroad while upon or above the stairway from the Bridge to its railroad platform, except from injuries caused solely by the acts of negligence of said "The Trustees" or their servants.

"The Company" further agrees that it will during the continuance of this lease, indemnify and save harmless "The Trustees," its agents and servants from all liability for accidents to persons or property arising anywhere on the premises hereby demised, from any negligence of the agents or servants of "The Company." "The Company" covenants that the premises occupied by it shall be kept clean at its expense, and to the satisfaction of the Engineer of "The Trustees."

Third—"The Trustees" license "The Company" to construct and maintain, at the expense of the latter, during the continuance of this agreement, the foot walk or gallery, extending from the Sands street terminal of "The Company" to the demised premises, the location and construction of such foot walk or gallery to be according to the plan hereto annexed, and to be approved of by the Engineer of "The Trustees."

Fourth—"The Trustees," so far as it has the power grants to "The Company" the right and easement to construct its proposed elevated railroad terminal station and tracks upon and over the plaza between High, Sands, Fulton and Washington streets. The number and position of the columns upon the plaza shall be substantially as shown upon the annexed plan.

In case it shall be found in construction that for engineering reasons the position of the columns should be different from those indicated upon the plan, they may be changed as required, provided the previous written approval of the Engineer of the Bridge shall have been obtained. All construction under this contract shall be according to the said plan hereto annexed, and in every respect such construction shall be to the full satisfaction of the Engineer of "The Trustees."

Fifth—This agreement is made for the convenience of the traveling public seeking and leaving the Bridge. "The Company" agrees to receive, discharge and distribute their passengers at the Brooklyn Bridge station in accordance with the regulations which may be made by "The Trustees" from time to time for the accommodation of the public.

IN WITNESS WHEREOF the parties hereto have caused these presents to be signed by their respective Presidents and Secretaries, and their corporate seal to be hereto affixed, the day and year first above written.

In presence of

SAM'L K. PROBASCO.

    THE KINGS COUNTY ELEVATED RAILWAY CO.,

[SEAL.]   By JAMES JOURDAN,
                                            President.

Attest:

  H. J. ROBINSON.
      Secretary.

THE TRUSTEES OF THE NEW YORK AND BROOKLYN BRIDGE.

[SEAL.]   JAMES HOWELL
                                            President.

HENRY BEAM,
    Secretary.

STATE OF NEW YORK, } ss.:
County of Kings,

On this ninth day of November, in the year eighteen hundred and ninety-four (1894), before me personally came and appeared James Howell, to me known and known to me to be the President of The Trustees of the New York and Brooklyn Bridge, who, being by me duly sworn, deposed and said that he is the President of said The Trustees of the New York and Brooklyn Bridge; that he resides in the City of Brooklyn; that he knows the corporate seal of said corporation; that the seal affixed to the foregoing instrument is such corporate seal, and that he affixed it thereto as President of the said corporation by authority of the Trustees of said corporation, and that he signed his name thereto as President by the like authority.

      HENRY BEAM,
       Notary Public,
        Kings County.

STATE OF NEW YORK, } ss.:
County of Kings,

On this eighth day of November, in the year eighteen hundred and ninety-four (1894), before me personally came and appeared James Jourdan, to me known and known to me to be the President of The Kings County Elevated Railway Company, who being by me duly sworn, did depose and say that he is the President of the said Company; that he resides in the City of Brooklyn; that he knows the corporate seal of said Company, and that the seal affixed to the foregoing instrument is such corporate seal, and that he affixed it thereto as President of the said corporation by authority of the Trustees of said Company, and that he signed his name thereto as President by the like authority.

      SAML. K. PROBASCO,
       Notary Public,
        Kings County.

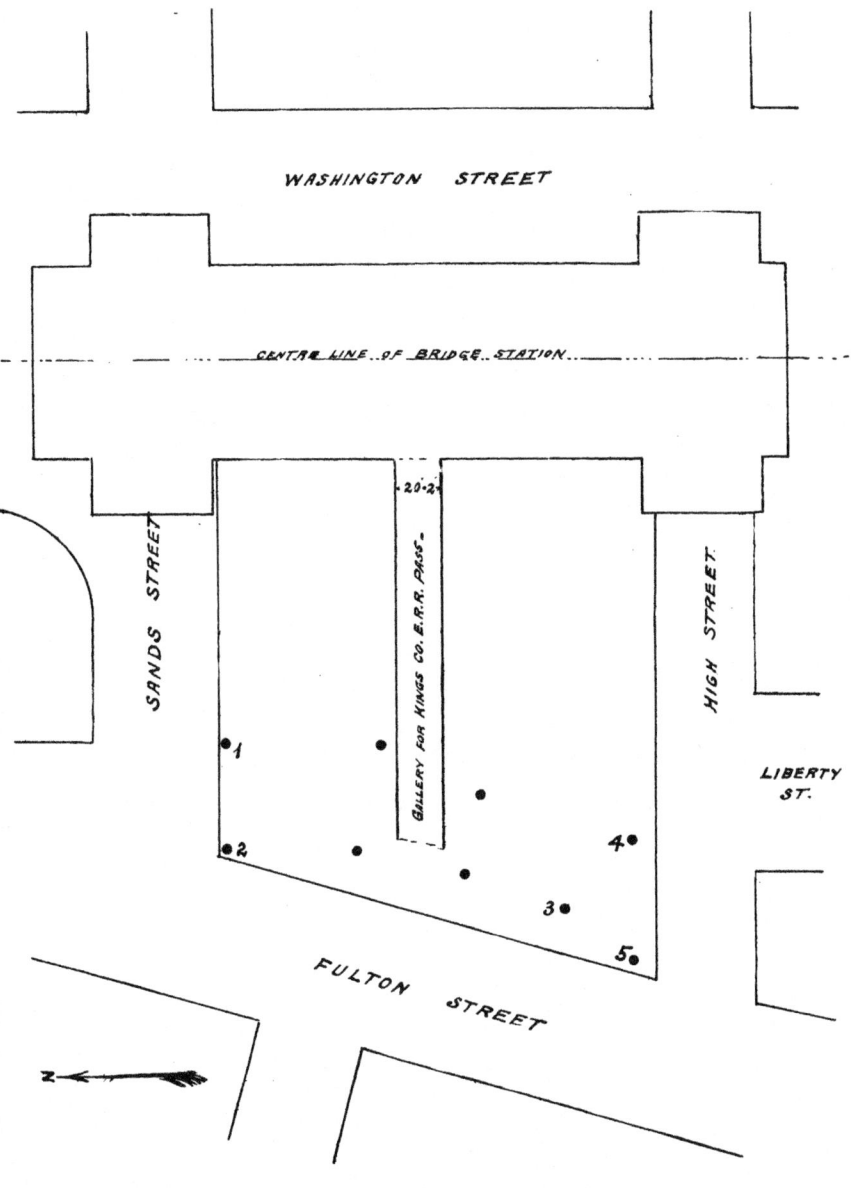

1, 2, 3, 4, 5 Scale: 1 inch = 50 feet.
Columns shown in diagram are for joint use of
Kings County and Brooklyn-Union-Seaside R.R. Companies

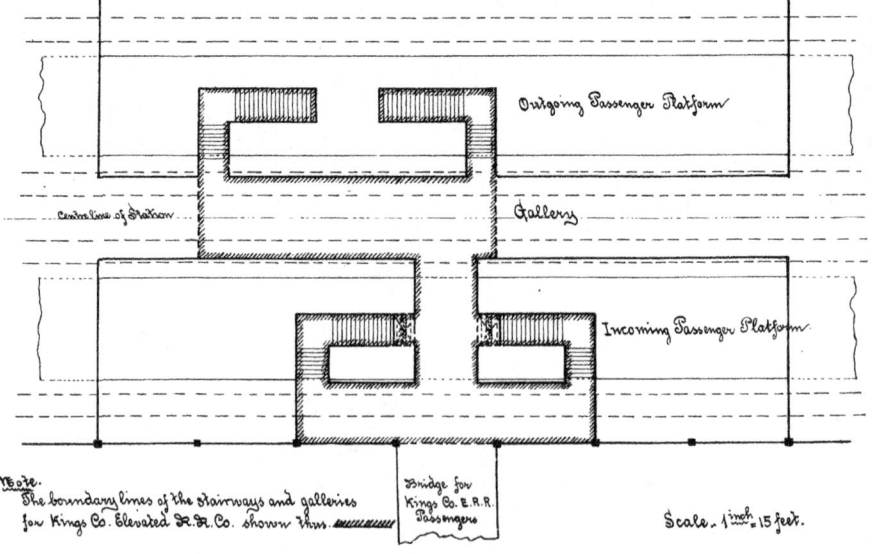

AGREEMENT.

THE BROOKLYN CITY & NEWTOWN RAILROAD CO.
WASHINGTON STREET SIDING.

MEMORANDUM OF AGREEMENT, made this 15th day of February, 1896, by and between THE TRUSTEES OF THE NEW YORK AND BROOKLYN BRIDGE, party of the first part, hereinafter called "THE TRUSTEES" and the BROOKLYN CITY AND NEWTOWN RAILROAD COMPANY, party of the second part, hereinafter called "THE RAILROAD COMPANY."

WHEREAS, "The Trustees" are authorized to improve the terminal facilities of the New York and Brooklyn Bridge, and are engaged in making such improvements, and among others in improving the connection between the Bridge and the railroad of "The Railroad Company."

NOW, THEREFORE, THIS AGREEMENT WITNESSETH: That "The Trustees" do hereby license and permit "The Railroad Company" to enter upon the lands acquired by the Trustees of the New York and Brooklyn Bridge for Bridge purposes between Sands and High streets and next to the Bridge passenger depot, and to construct terminal tracks and to operate the railroad of "The Railroad Company" during the pleasure of "The Trustees," at the yearly license fee or sum of five hundred dollars, to be paid in two equal semi-annual payments on the 20th days of February and August in each and every year.

"The Railroad Company" covenants that it will remove its tracks from the lands aforesaid, abandon the operation of its railroad upon notice of three months from "The Trustees" requiring such removal and abandonment, and thereupon that it will restore the lands to their present condition.

"The Railroad Company" further covenants to make its construction according to the plan or diagram hereunto annexed, made part hereof, and that such construction and subsequent operation shall be to the satisfaction of "The Trustees."

"The Trustees" reserve all right to make ordinances for the regulation of the premises in question and the use thereof, under the laws relating to the New York and Brooklyn Bridge, and authorizing the enactment of ordinances by ": The Trustees."

IN WITNESS WHEREOF, the parties have caused these presents to be signed by their Presidents and their respective seals to be hereunto affixed the day and year first above written.

   TRUSTEES NEW YORK AND BROOKLYN BRIDGE,

           JAMES HOWELL,
              President.

[SEAL.]

Attest:
 HENRY BEAM,
   Secretary,

   BROOKLYN CITY AND NEWTOWN R. R. Co.,

      By JOHN N. PARTRIDGE,
           President.

[SEAL.]

Attest:
 DUNCAN B. CANNON,
   Secretary.

STATE OF NEW YORK, }
 City of Brooklyn, } ss.:
 County of Kings,   }

On this 17th day of February, 1896, before me came James Howell, with whom I am personally acquainted, who being by me duly sworn, says that he resides in The City of New York, and is the President of The Trustees of the New York and Brooklyn Bridge above named; that he knows the corporate seal of said corporation; that the seal affixed to the foregoing instrument is such corporate seal; that it was affixed by order of the Board of Trustees of said corporation, and that he signed his name thereto as President by the like authority and direction.

      GEORGE V. S. WILLIAMS,
[SEAL.]   Notary Public,
          Kings County.

STATE OF NEW YORK,
   City of Brooklyn, } *ss.:*
   County of Kings,

On this 15th day of February, 1896, before me came John N. Partridge, with whom I am personally acquainted, who being by me duly sworn, says that he resides in the City of Brooklyn, and is the President of the Brooklyn City and Newtown Railroad Company above named; that he knows the corporate seal of said company; that the seal affixed to the foregoing instrument is such corporate seal; that it was affixed by order of the Board of Directors of said company, and that he signed his name thereto as President by the like authority and direction.

                         S. H. WILKINS,
[SEAL.]   Notary Public,
                               Kings County.

Oversized Foldout

AGREEMENT.

THE NASSAU ELECTRIC RAILROAD COMPANY.
WASHINGTON STREET SIDING.

MEMORANDUM OF AGREEMENT, made this second day of July, 1896, by and between THE TRUSTEES OF THE NEW YORK AND BROOKLYN BRIDGE, party of the first part, hereinafter called the "TRUSTEES," and THE NASSAU ELECTRIC RAILROAD COMPANY, party of the second part, hereinafter called the "RAILROAD COMPANY."

WHEREAS, The "Trustees" are authorized to improve the terminal facilities of the New York and Brooklyn Bridge, and are engaged in making such improvements, and among others in improving the connection between the Bridge and the railroad of the "Railroad Company,"

NOW, THEREFORE, THIS AGREEMENT WITNESSETH: That the "Trustees" do hereby license and permit the "Railroad Company" to enter upon the lands acquired by the "Trustees" of the New York and Brooklyn Bridge for bridge purposes in the City of Brooklyn, on the westerly side of Washington street between the southerly side of High street and the northerly side of Concord street and adjoining the sidewalk as the same now exists along the westerly side of Washington street between the points aforesaid, and to construct its track and operate the railroad of the said "Railroad Company" by electric power during the pleasure of the "Trustees," at the yearly license fee or sum of One Thousand Dollars, to be paid in four equal quarterly payments on the first days of October, January, April and July in each and every year.

The "Railroad Company" covenants, that it will remove its track from the lands aforesaid, abandon the operation of its track upon notice of three months from the "Trustees" requiring such removal and abandonment, and thereupon that it will restore the lands and street where such track shall be located to their present condition at the sole cost and expense of said "Railroad Company."

The "Railroad Company" further covenants to make its construction and locate, maintain and keep its track in the position and location shown upon and according to the plan or diagram hereunto annexed and made part hereof, upon which plan the track of the "Railroad Company" so to be located, constructed and maintained is marked with the words: "Track of The Nassau Electric Railroad Company," located by C. C. Martin, Chief Engineer, and that it will in such construction and location follow the directions of the Chief Engineer of the party of the first part upon the lines to be staked out by him, and that such construction and subsequent operation shall be to the satisfaction of the "Trustees."

It is hereby especially covenanted and agreed by and between the parties hereto, that under no circumstances shall the "Railroad Company" so construct or maintain its track as to reduce or diminish the space or headroom between the surface of Washington street and Nassau street at the crossing of said streets and the structure of the "Trustees" over the same, and that should the surface of such streets at such crossing be hereafter lowered by action of the authorities of the City of Brooklyn that the said "Railroad Company" will conform the construction of its track to such lowering, and place and construct and maintain the same upon the surface of the said crossing as thus lowered, and should such lowering occur after the track of the Railroad is constructed, that the Railroad will change and lower its track in conformity with the provisions of this instrument, at its own cost and without expense to the "Trustees."

The "Trustees" reserve all right to make ordinances for the regulation of the premises in question and the use thereof under the laws relating to the New York and Brooklyn Bridge, and authorizing the enactment of ordinances by the "Trustees."

IN WITNESS WHEREOF, The parties have caused these presents to be signed by their Presidents, and their respective seals to be hereunto affixed, the day and year first above written.

NASSAU ELECTRIC RAILROAD COMPANY,

[SEAL.] By A. L. JOHNSON,
President.

Attest:
 JAMES CHURCH,
  Secretary.

TRUSTEES, NEW YORK AND BROOKLYN BRIDGE,

By JAMES HOWELL,
President.

[SEAL.]

Attest:
 HENRY BEAM,
  Secretary.

STATE OF NEW YORK, } ss.:
 County of Kings,

On this 2d day of July, 1896, before me came James Howell, with whom I am personally acquainted, who being by me duly sworn says that he resides in the City of Brooklyn and is the President of The Trustees of the New York and Brooklyn Bridge, above named; that he knows the corporate seal of said corporation; that the seal affixed to the foregoing instrument is such corporate seal; that it was affixed by order of the Board of Trustees of said corporation, and that he signed his name thereto as President by the like authority and direction.

HENRY BEAM,
Notary Public,
Kings County.

STATE OF NEW YORK, } ss.:
County of Kings,

On this 2d day of July, 1896, before me came Albert L. Johnson, with whom I am personally acquainted, who, being by me duly sworn, says that he resides in the City of Brooklyn and is the President of The Nassau Electric Railroad Company, above named; that he knows the corporate seal of said Company; that the seal affixed to the foregoing instrument is such corporate seal; that it was affixed by order of the Board of Trustees of said Company, and that he signed his name thereto as President by the like authority and direction.

CHARLES W. CHURCH, JR.,
Notary Public,
Kings County.

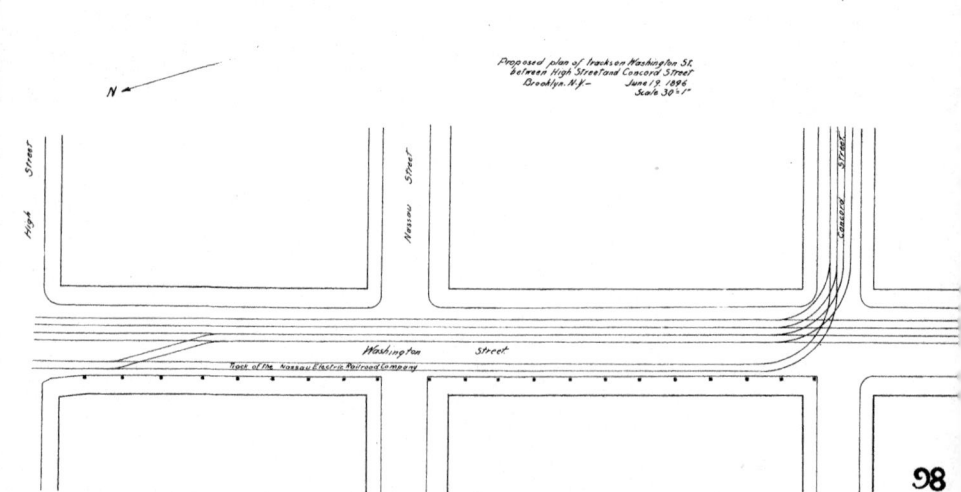

AGREEMENT

TRUSTEES OF THE NEW YORK AND BROOKLYN BRIDGE

AND

BROOKLYN HEIGHTS RAILROAD COMPANY

August 23, 1897.

THIS AGREEMENT, made this 23d day of August, 1897, between THE TRUSTEES OF THE NEW YORK AND BROOKLYN BRIDGE, party of the first part, and THE BROOKLYN HEIGHTS RAILROAD COMPANY, party of the second part, WITNESSETH:

That the party of the first part, for and in consideration of the payments to be made to it by the party of the second part, and of the faithful, just and full performance of the undertakings, covenants and agreements to be by the said party of the second part performed and carried out as hereinafter set forth, doth, subject to the conditions and restrictions herein provided and expressed, grant and lease to the party of the second part the right and privilege to enter upon the premises of the party of the first part with its cars for the transportation of passengers, and to transport the cars of the said party of the second part and the passengers using and traveling in said cars across its Bridge, subject, however, in all things to the control and direction of the Chief Engineer of the party of the first part.

And the terms upon which this lease, license, privilege or grant is made, the conditions subject to which the rights hereby conferred upon the party of the second part are to be exercised, and the covenants by said party of the second part to be observed and performed are as follows, to wit:

First—The party of the second part shall arrange for the use of a single track for passing from the City of Brooklyn to The

City of New York, which track shall be located on the north side of the north roadway of the said The New York and Brooklyn Bridge; and for the use of a single track for passing from the City of New York to the City of Brooklyn, which track shall be located on the south side of the south roadway of the said The New York and Brooklyn Bridge; and for tracks at or beyond the present terminals of the said The New York and Brooklyn Bridge in the City of New York, sufficient and proper for the purpose of connecting the said two above-mentioned tracks, which connecting tracks shall be so located, placed, situated, constructed and used as shall in nowise interfere with the use and operation by the Trustees of The New York and Brooklyn Bridge of its railroad upon and across the said premises of the said Trustees.

The cars of the said party of the second part shall be operated and propelled across the said Bridge by electric power, to be supplied by the said Railroad Company.

Said Railroad Company shall prepare the plans and do and pay for the work, provided only that said plans shall be approved by the Chief Engineer of the party of the first part, and the work be carried on subject to his approval and inspection, and such plans are those hereto attached, and which it is hereby covenanted are and constitute a part of this agreement.

Second—The location of the said tracks and of all curves and of all switches, sidings, platforms and constructions of every kind necessary to the use of said tracks on the said Bridge, its approaches and terminals, shall be under the absolute control and direction of the Chief Engineer of said Bridge, and no construction of any kind connected therewith or relating thereto shall be had or used unless the plan or plans for the same have been first submitted to the said Engineer and have been approved by him, and are hereto attached as aforesaid.

Third—The said Trustees, the party of the first part, shall permit the said Railroad Company, together with any other surface railroad company, should privileges similar to those herein contained be extended by the said party of the first part to any other surface railroad company, to construct a platform, elevators and stairs at the New York terminal of said Bridge for the use of said railroad companies and their passengers. Said platform, elevators and stairways shall be constructed at such point as shall be designated by the Chief Engineer of the party of the first part. The party of the second part, either alone or together with any other surface railroad company to whom privileges similar to those herein contained shall be extended, shall prepare the plans and do and pay for the work of such construction, provided always that said plans shall be approved by the Chief Engineer of the party of the first part, and the work be carried on subject to his approval and inspection, and which plans are hereto attached as aforesaid.

Fourth—The expense of all changes and additions necessary in the construction upon said Bridge, or the approach thereto, in order to permit the operation of said cars and the construction of said tracks between New York and Brooklyn and connecting tracks heretofore mentioned, and of all other tracks, switches, platforms, elevators and appliances of every kind and nature required in connection therewith, and the repair and maintenance thereof, and the expense of operating said elevators shall be borne and paid for by the party of the second part. And the cost of whatever part of such changes, additions and construction, track and tracks, platforms and appliances of every kind and nature, and of the repair and maintenance thereof, and the expense of operating said elevators which shall be used by more than one surface railroad company, or the necessity for the creation of which shall be common to the bringing upon the Bridge of the cars of more than one surface railroad company, shall be borne by the several railroad companies to whom privileges similar to those herein set forth shall be extended, in such shares and proportions as they may agree upon, or, if they fail to agree, in such shares and proportions as the Trustees, the said party of the first part, may determine. All plans, contracts for labor and material necessary to the construction aforesaid, and to the additions and changes and tracks aforesaid, and to the entry upon the said premises of the Trustees, and the use and construction of tracks upon said premises, and the use of the tracks upon and over said premises by said Railroad Company, shall be made by said Railroad Company in its own name and upon its own responsibility; all material necessary to be used upon the said premises of Trustees shall be supplied by said Railroad Company, and any and all labor to be performed upon said premises shall be performed by said Railroad Company, and the cost thereof paid by said Railroad Company, before entering said premises of said Trustees with its cars.

All rights of way, franchises and property necessary to be secured in order to construct the tracks upon which to enter upon and leave the said Bridge property shall be secured and paid for by the said Railroad Company in the manner hereinbefore provided.

Provided, only, that if privileges similar to those herein set forth and expressed be extended to surface railroad companies, other than the party of the second part, then, and in that event, the contracts hereinbefore referred to shall be entered into by all of said surface railroads, jointly, and upon their joint responsibility, and the said material shall be supplied at the joint cost of said surface railroads, and the cost of the labor to be performed upon the said premises of the said party of the first part shall, likewise, be at the joint cost of said surface railroads, the proportions of which shall, if not agreed upon by and between the said railroads, be determined and fixed as to each by the said Trustees, and from such determination there shall, on the part of said railroads, be no appeal.

All of such work and material shall be subject to approval and rejection by the said Trustees. All of such construction upon property belonging to the said Trustees of The New York and Brooklyn Bridge shall become and be the property of the said Trustees of the said New York and Brooklyn Bridge when and as soon as work shall be begun or material necessary to such construction shall be delivered upon the premises of the party of the first part. All work done in pursuance of the terms of this contract by said Railroad Company shall be so carried on as in no manner to interfere with, limit or obstruct the operation by said party of the first part of its railroad across said Bridge, and in such manner as not to interfere with, limit or obstruct the use of the roadways of said Bridge by the public in any manner so as to reduce the use of each of said roadways to be left clear for public use to less than ten feet.

The party of the first part doth hereby covenant and agree that should privileges similar to those herein referred to be extended to any stieet or surface railroad company other than those entering into contracts with said party of the first part similar to and executed simultaneously with the execution of this instrument at any time subsequent to the completion of the work herein and hereby contemplated and provided for, such privileges shall be so extended upon terms similar to those herein set forth, and upon further terms that all such further companies shall be required to pay to said party of the first part an amount equal to the proportion of the cost of the work, material and labor and herein provided for, which such company would have been compelled to pay had it been one of the companies originally entering into the agreements similar to this one, which payments shall be apportioned in the same manner that the pro rata cost shall be apportioned among such original companies, but to which there shall be added interest upon such amount so fixed from the time of the last payment by original companies.

And said party of the first part doth covenant that, upon receipt of such payment from such subsequently admitted companies, it will distribute the same among the original companies in the same proportions as the payment made by them shall bear to the said whole cost.

Fifth—The said Trustees shall have full and complete power to make and adopt all rules and regulations which to them shall seem reasonable and proper relating to the operation of the cars of said Railroad Company over said Bridge, and the operation of its elevators and of every other railroad company to which privileges similar to those herein granted may be extended, including the method of payment of tolls, the rate of speed of said cars, the movement and headway thereof, the style of cars to be used and the condition thereof, the switching of cars and the use of platforms, and governing and controlling all of the electrical equipment for operating the cars of said Railroad Company upon and across the said Bridge, which before being installed, and while being maintained, shall, at all times, be subject to approval by the Chief Engineer of the said party of the first part, and to amend or alter any such rules or regulations so as to secure the safety and comfort of persons using the said Bridge, and to subserve the purposes for which the said Bridge was constructed. But the Railroad Company shall be allowed to place and retain advertising signs inside its cars.

The Railroad Company shall not bring upon the premises of the party of the first part, or deliver to them for transportation across the Bridge, any cars in which smoking shall be permitted while the cars of the said Railroad Company are upon the premises of the party of the first part.

Sixth—All cars used on the Bridge service and all equipment and appliances relating thereto located on Bridge property shall be subject at all times to inspection by the Bridge authorities, who shall have power to forbid rights on the Bridge to cars that may, for any reason, be unsatisfactory, and to direct the removal of any old or inadequate equipment or appliances, and the substitution therefor for others of approved character.

Seventh—The said Railroad Company shall pay to the said Trustees of The New York and Brooklyn Bridge the sum of five per cent per round trip for each car operated or transported by said company across said Bridge; provided that, pursuant to the provisions of Chapter 663, Laws 1897, the said party of the second part shall not by reason of the payments by it to be made to the party of the first part as herein provided or otherwise, or for any reason whatever, " charge any
" fare in excess of, or additional to, the fare exacted by it from
" any passenger for one continuous ride upon any of its routes
" in either of the cities of New York or Brooklyn, as the case
" may be, so that the said route of said Corporation operated
" across said Bridge hereunder, so far as the exaction of a
" fare is concerned, shall be taken and deemed to be a part of
" the continuous route, or one of the continuous routes, of
" the said Railroad Corporation whereon one fare is exacted,
" so that no extra or additional fare shall be exacted by said
" party of the second part from any passenger carried to or
" from the Bridge and across the Bridge in addition to the
" fare exacted from such passenger for carriage to and from
" the Bridge only."

Eighth—The said Railroad Company shall protect and hold harmless the said Trustee from and against all losses, damages and claims for damages, actions, recoveries, costs, disbursements and expenses of every nature arising from, based upon, connected with, or in any manner charged to be due to injury to person or property received or sustained by any person upon and in the cars of the said company whenever and wherever upon the premises of said Trustees such injuries may arise, be received or sustained, or which may be caused by the cars of the said Railroad Company, or which may arise from or be connected with the presence and operation of such cars upon such premises or which shall in anywise be connected with or arise out of the bringing of the said cars upon the premises of the party of the first part, or transporting or operating them upon, over or across the same, or which may arise from or be connected with the making, building, constructing, erecting or changing of any work, of every kind necessary for the bringing of the cars of the party of the second part upon the said Bridge, and the operating and the transporting of the same across the said Bridge, or in any and every wise growing out of the use of the said Bridge and any of the premises, appurtenances and appliances thereunto belonging, by the party of the second part.

And the said Railroad Company shall further protect and hold harmless the said Trustees from and against losses, damages and claims for damages, actions, recoveries, costs, disbursements and expenses of every nature which may arise or result from any failure or delay on the part of the said Railroad Company to promptly and regularly operate and transport its cars across said Bridge in either direction, or for any delay or hindrance to said cars while in transit, from whatever cause or reason such neglect or refusal or delay may arise, or which may arise to any person using the said Bridge in any way or manner who shall be injured in person or property, or hindered or delayed in the use of said Bridge by reason of any matter, thing or occurrence arising from or connected with the operation of the cars across the said structure. And should there at any time occur a block upon the roadway of said Bridge, or interference with the use of said roadway by the public by reason of the operation of the cars of the said Railroad Company across the Bridge, the said Railroad Company shall protect and hold harmless the said Trustees from and against all claims or damages resulting from the same. And should there be caused by the operation of the said cars, or in any way connected therewith, any accident upon such roadway, or elsewhere, the said Railroad Company shall in like manner protect and hold harmless the said Trustees against losses, damages, and claims for damages, actions, recoveries, costs, disbursements and expenses of every nature, which may arise therefrom.

And the said Railroad Company shall further protect and hold harmless said Trustees from and against any and all suits, lets, hindrances, actions, recoveries, claims, damages, costs, disbursements and expenses of every kind, nature, amount and description, which may arise, be made and presented, brought, instituted, sustained or recovered on the ground of deprivation of owners of property adjoining premises of the party of the first part of light or air, or interruption of either, or of damages of any and every nature consequent upon and resulting from the bringing of the cars of said Railroad upon premises of party of the first part and operating the same thereupon, and over said premises and Bridge.

Ninth—The supervision, management and control of the cars of the Railroad Company shall in every particular and at all times be wholly exercised by the Trustees of The New York and Brooklyn Bridge, within the discretion and at the dictation of the Chief Engineer of said Trustees from the entering of said cars upon the premises of said Trustees to the departure of said cars from said premises, and the said Chief Engineer shall at all times regulate and limit in his discretion the number of cars of the said company which may be operated as aforesaid. But the total number of cars so operated at any one time by all the surface railroad corporations entitled so to operate the same, shall be apportioned as nearly as practicable between such companies so that the number of cars permitted to be so operated by each company shall bear the same proportion to the total number so operated by all such companies, as the cost of construction borne by such railroad company in pursuance of the Fourth Article hereof shall bear to the total cost thereof borne by all such companies.

All employees of the party of the second part, motormen, conductors and others employed in connection with the operation of the cars of the party of the second part, upon and over the premises of the party of the first part, and in connection with service to be rendered by the party of the second part upon the said Bridge, shall be of good character, skilled in their respective kinds of work, and satisfactory to the Trustees of the Bridge, the party of the first part hereto, and there shall be and hereby is reserved to the said Trustees the right to be exercised by the Chief Engineer of the said party of the first part to refuse to permit any such employees not satisfactory to said Trustees to enter upon said premises, and to expel from said premises at any time at his discretion any such employee who is not so satisfactory.

AND WHEREAS, it is in contemplation by and between the parties to this agreement that privileges similar to those herein contained and expressed are to be extended by the said Trustees, the party of the first part, to surface railroad corporations other than the party of the second part hereto; therefore, it is further provided and agreed that the use of all tracks, constructions, changes, additions, platforms, stairways, appurtenances and appliances whatsoever upon the premises of the said party of the first part may be by them granted, leased and extended to such other railroad companies upon such terms, and subject to such conditions as may be by said Trustees imposed; and especially that in the joint use of the said tracks and appurtenances hereinbefore mentioned the Chief Engineer of the party of the first part shall have and exercise full, unlimited arbitrary control and power as to the total number of cars of all of said various railroad companies to be permitted to enter upon the said premises and use the appliances thereof, which total number of cars shall be apportioned between the different companies as aforesaid, and provide all rules and regulations which, in his judgment, may be expedient and necessary to promulgate and enforce with reference thereto.

Tenth—The term of the right and privilege hereby granted to the party of the second part to enter upon the premises of the party of the first part with its cars for the transportation of passengers and to transport its cars and the passengers using and traveling in the same across its Bridge, and to that end to cross, intersect, join and unite its railroad with the railroad operated by the party of the first part, shall be terminable at the option of either party hereto after expiration of ten years from the date when this contract shall be duly executed, provided only that if, in the opinion of the party of the first part, or its legal successors, and of the Mayor of The City of New York, and of the President of the Borough of Brooklyn, to be hereafter elected, pursuant to the provisions of chapter 378 of the Laws of 1897, or in the opinion of the majority of them, it should be determined that it is against the public interest to continue the operation of the trains or cars of the party of the second part upon, over and across the Bridge, or if the said party of the second part should for itself determine that the facilities afforded it are inadequate for its passenger service, then, and in that event, this agreement and all of the rights and privileges granted to said party of the second part and obligations assumed by it, shall be terminable on and after three months' notice in writing by either party to the other that it elects to determine said contract.

Eleventh—The said Roalroad Company before entering in any manner upon the premises of the party of the first part for the performance of any work necessary to make the connections, additions and changes hereinbefore provided for or for the construction of the tracks and railroad hereby contemplated, and the appliances and appurtenances to be used in connection therewith, shall execute and deliver to the Trustees of said Bridge, the party of the first part, its bond in the sum of One Hundred Thousand Dollars and in such form and with such sureties as the said Trustees shall prescribe (which bond shall be approved as to form and manner of execution by Counsel for the said Trustees), conditioned that said Company shall promptly complete the work entered upon by it as heretofore provided, and that if it shall fail so to do that it shall pay to said Trustee of said Bridge the necessary expenses of completing the same or of removing the whole or any portion of such work, structure, connections, changes, additions, tracks, platform, elevators, stairways, appurtenances and appliances which are or may be upon the property of the said Trustees of the New York and Brooklyn Bridge, and of restoring the said Bridge and all the premises of the party of the first part, and all things appurtenant thereto, to its and their present condition, whichever the said Trustees shall elect to do; and further conditioned that the said Railroad Company shall observe, obey and keep each and every rule and regulation made and adopted by the said Trustees as hereinbefore provided, and for the discharge of any and all liability hereby imposed and which may arise or be incurred pursuant to the provisions of this contract; and further conditioned that the said Railroad Company shall and will faithfully, promptly and fully pay to said Trstees the rental reserved and the charges hereby imposed.

And for a failure and neglect to observe, obey and keep such rules and regulations, or any of them, and for a failure to promptly make payment to said Trustees of the rental reserved and of the charges by this agreement imposed, the said Trustees may revoke the said agreement, so far as it affects the said Railroad Company, and, thereupon said Railroad Company shall forfeit all rights and privileges theretofore enjoyed thereunder.

Twelfth—It is hereby covenanted, agreed and understood that the foregoing license, grant and agreement, in all its parts, does, and is intended to apply to the
Railroad Company, party of the second part, and to any and all the legal successors of said Company and of and to its rights, privileges and franchises.

Thirteenth—The said Railroad Company doth hereby further covenant, promise and agree that for and in consideration of the provisions of this instrument and of the privileges and grants thereby extended to it by the party of the first part, it will commence the work preparatory to the exercise of the privileges hereby extended within ten days after the date of the execution of this instrument, and that all of the said work hereinbefore provided for as necessary to the operation of the cars of the said Railroad Company over the Bridge shall be fully completed, and said operation of cars be regularly commenced within six months after the date of the execution of these presents, provided only, that should either the commencement, continuation or finishing of such work or the operation of the cars of the said Railroad Company upon, over and across the premises of the party of the first part be delayed by litigation, strikes or causes of delay not created by the party of the second part, and not to be avoided by ordinary precautions on its part, the time necessarily consumed in such litigation and by such strikes or causes of delay aforesaid, shall be added to the time herein provided for the beginning and completion of the work aforesaid, and further provided that for failure to comply with this provision of this agreement, or by reason of the institution by or at the instigation of the said Railroad Company of litigation of any nature, instituted in any wise for the purpose of increasing the time within which the provisions of this contract shall be put in effect, the said party of the first part may, at the discretion of this Board of Trustees, revoke each and every privilege hereinbefore contained and set forth, and upon such revocation all work and material put upon the premises of the party of the first part by the said Railroad Company shall be and become forfeited to the Trustees without damage or compensation therefor to the said Railroad Company.

It is hereby covenanted and agreed, that the said Railroad Company shall not in any way enter upon the premises of the party of the first part or commence any work or construction thereon, nor place any material to be used in such work and construction upon the premises of the party of the first part until all the work and construction to be undertaken and performed by the party of the second part outside of the property of the said Trustees, and necessary and sufficient for the purpose of making the connection between the railroad of the said party of the second part and that of the said Trustees, as hereinbefore provided, shall be fairly under way to the end that all construction necessary to cross the Bridge by cars of the aforesaid railroad may be completed at about the same time; nor shall said Railroad Company enter upon or do any work of construction upon the premises of said Trustees until it shall have secured its right of way and removed any and every injunction that may have been granted by a Court of competent jurisdiction.

And also that the said Railroad Company shall not in any way interfere with the operation of the railroad operated by the Trustees, pending construction necessary to connect the railroad of the party of the second part with the Bridge, and permit its cars to be operated thereon, nor shall said railroad company use the structure of the Bridge for the storage of material to be used in such work and construction, nor permit its employees, or the employees of contractors, to use the Bridge premises as a rendezvous or resting-place, but work of construction is to proceed day by day without interruption, except if the railroad company is enjoined from proceeding by the Court, or in the event of strikes, or hindrances, or delays beyond the control of the railroad Company, and it is expressly stipulated that in all matters connected with construction and work on the premises of the Trustees, that the Chief Engineer of the Bridge shall have absolute supervision and control.

IN WITNESS WHEREOF, the parties hereto have caused these presents to be subscribed by their respective Presidents and their respective corporate seals to be hereto affixed this twenty-third day of August, A. D., eighteen hundred and ninety-seven.

(Signed) TRUSTEES, NEW YORK AND BROOKLYN BRIDGE,
In presence of:
By WILLIAM BERRI,
President.

[L. S.]
Attest:
  HENRY BEAM,
    Secretary.

BROOKLYN HEIGHTS RAILROAD COMPANY,
By C. L. ROSSITER,
President.

[L. S.]
  T. S. WILLIAMS,
    Secretary.

STATE OF NEW YORK, }
  City of Brooklyn, } *ss.:*
  County of Kings, }

On this twenty-third day of August, in the year eighteen hundred and ninety-seven, before me personally came William Berri, to me personally known, who being by me duly sworn, did depose and say: That he resided in the City of Brooklyn; that he was the President of the Trustees of The New York and Brooklyn Bridge, the corporation described in and which executed the foregoing instrument; that he knew the corporate seal of the said The Trustees of the New York and Brooklyn Bridge; that the seal affixed to the foregoing instrument was such corporate seal; that it was affixed by order of said Trustees and that he signed his name thereto as President by the like order.

    (Signed)   A. F. BRITTON,
                                    Notary Public,
                                        Kings County.

STATE OF NEW YORK, }
  City of Brooklyn, } *ss.:*
  County of Kings, }

On this twenty-third day of August, in the year eighteen hundred and ninety-seven, before me personally came C. L. Rossiter, to me personally known, who being by me duly sworn, did depose and say: That he resided in the City of Brooklyn; that he was the President of The Brooklyn Heights Railroad Company, the corporation described in and which executed the foregoing instrument; that he knew the corporate seal of the said railroad company; that the seal affixed to the foregoing instrument was such corporate seal; that it was affixed by order of the Board of Directors of the said Brooklyn Heights Railroad Company, and that he signed his name thereto by the like order as President of the said.

    (Signed)   A. F. BRITTON,
                                    Notary Public,
                                        Kings County.

33

SUPPLEMENTARY AGREEMENT

TRUSTEES OF THE NEW YORK AND BROOKLYN BRIDGE

AND

BROOKLYN HEIGHTS R. R. CO.

SEPTEMBER 29, 1897.

THIS AGREEMENT, made this 29th day of September, 1897, between THE TRUSTEES OF THE NEW YORK AND BROOKLYN BRIDGE, party of the first part, and THE BROOKLYN HEIGHTS RAILROAD COMPANY, party of the second part, WITNESSETH, that,

WHEREAS, a certain agreement made and entered into by and between the parties hereto, dated the 23d day of August, 1897, provides for a grant by the party of the first part to the party of the second part of a right and license to enter upon the premises of the party of the first part with its cars, and to have the same and the passengers using the same transported across the Bridge of the party of the first part to and fro between the cities of Brooklyn and New York and for the exit from the premises of the party of the first part with said cars and passengers upon various and sundry conditions in said agreement set forth, in and by which agreement it is specifically provided that one of said conditions is that all entry upon and use of the premises of the party of the first part shall be upon plans to be made and submitted by the party of the second part and approved by the engineer of the party of the first part and attached to and forming part of said contract, and

WHEREAS, in accordance with the provisions of said contract, plans were duly submitted, approved and attached to said agreement of August 23d prior to the execution thereof, and upon the execution thereof became part and parcel of said agreement, and

WHEREAS, it has been since the execution of the said agreement of August 23d mutually arranged, consented to, agreed and stipulated by and between the parties hereto that the said contract of August 23d shall be modified in that there shall be certain changes made in the plans above mentioned and referred to, but that no other right, privilege, license, covenant, stipulation, agreement, condition or provision of the said agreement shall in any wise be changed, but that each and every thereof shall be maintained in full force, virtue and effect,

NOW THEREFORE, IT IS HEREBY COVENANTED AND AGREED,

That the plans hereto attached, made and submitted by the party of the second part and approved by the Chief Engineer of the party of the first part, shall be and hereby are upon execution of these presents substituted for the plans attached to the said agreement of August 23d, 1897, with like force and effect as though the plans hereto attached had been the original plans referred to in said agreement of August 23d, 1897, and that from and after the date of the execution of this instrument the said agreement of August 23d, 1897, shall be and is changed, altered and modified in so far as the change of plans and modification has been affected by the change of plans herein set forth.

AND, WHEREAS, the change of plans, made, submitted and approved as aforesaid and by this instrument effected and made a part of said agreement of August 23, as hereby modified, necessarily results in certain verbal changes in the said agreement of August 23, 1897; it is hereby further covenanted and agreed, that the aforesaid agreement shall in the following particulars be modified and changed as herein set forth.

The track which by paragraph "First" of said agreement was to be located on the north side of the north roadway shall be located instead on the south side of the north roadway and the track which by the same paragraph of said agreement was to be located on the south side of the south roadway shall be located on the north side of the south roadway.

In the third paragraph of said agreement the word "elevators" twice occurring therein is in each case to be struck out and the word "subways" in each case to be substituted.

In the fourth line of paragraph " Fourth " of said agreement the word " elevators " is to be struck out and the word " subway " substituted.

In the fifth and sixth and in the eighth and ninth lines of said paragraph the words " and the expense of operating said elevators " are to be struck out.

In paragraph " Fifth " the fourth line the words " and the operation of its elevators " are to be struck out.

And the said agreement of August 23, 1897, as so modified and changed, shall be of the same force and effect as if the changes here agreed to be made therein had been made before the said agreement of August 23, 1897, had been executed and as if the plans hereto attached had been attached to said agreement at the time of its execution and delivery in the place and stead of the plans which were originally attached thereto.

IN WITNESS WHEREOF, the parties hereto have caused these presents to be signed by their respective Presidents and their respective seals to be hereunto attached, the day and year first above written.

THE TRUSTEES OF THE NEW YORK AND BROOKLYN BRIDGE,
[SEAL.] By WILLIAM BERRI,
President.

Attest:
  HENRY BEAM,
      Secretary.

THE BROOKLYN HEIGHTS RAILROAD COMPANY,
By C. L. ROSSITER,
President.

[SEAL.]
Attest:
  T. S. WILLIAMS,
      Secretary.

STATE OF NEW YORK, } ss.:
County of Kings,

On this 14th day of October, 1897, before me personally came William Berri, to me known and with whom I am personally acquainted, who being by me duly sworn, did depose and say: That he resides at 401 Grand avenue, and is the President of the Board of Trustees of the New York and Brooklyn Bridge, the corporation described in and which executed the foregoing instrument as party of the first part; that he knows the corporate seal of said corporation; that the seal affixed to the foregoing instrument is such corporate seal, and was affixed thereto by order of the Board of Trustees of said Company, and that he signed his name thereto as President by the like authority and direction.

HENRY BEAM,
[SEAL.]   Notary Public,
Kings Co.

STATE OF NEW YORK, } ss.:
County of Kings,

On this 29th day of September, 1897, before me personally came Clinton L. Rossiter, to me known and with whom I am personally acquainted, who being by me duly sworn, did depose and say: That he resides at the City of Brooklyn and is the President of The Brooklyn Heights Railroad Company, the corporation described in and which executed the foregoing instrument as party of the second part; that he knows the corporate seal of said corporation; that the seal affixed to the foregoing instrument is such corporate seal, and was affixed thereto by order of the Board of Directors of said Company, and that he signed his name thereto as President by the like authority and direction.

A. L. BROUGHAM,
Com'r of Deeds,
City of Brooklyn.

AGREEMENT

ASSOCIATED TROLLEY COMPANIES
RELATIVE TO OPERATION OVER THE NEW YORK AND BROOKLYN BRIDGE.

AUGUST 23, 1897

THIS AGREEMENT, made this 23d day of August, 1897, between THE BROOKLYN HEIGHTS RAILROAD COMPANY and THE BROOKLYN, QUEENS COUNTY AND SUBURBAN RAILROAD COMPANY, parties of the first part; NASSAU ELECTRIC RAILROAD COMPANY, party of the second part; THE BROOKLYN CITY AND NEWTOWN RAILROAD COMPANY, party of the third part; and THE CONEY ISLAND AND BROOKLYN RAILROAD COMPANY, party of the fourth part, WITNESSETH:

WHEREAS, each of the said railroad companies, except the Brooklyn, Queens County and Suburban Railroad Company, has this day entered into a contract with the Trustees of The New York and Brooklyn Bridge for the operation of its cars over said Bridge in pursuance of plans attached to such contract, all of said contracts being of the same general tenor, and each set of said plans being the same.

NOW, THEREFORE, it is agreed that all expenditures heretofore incurred with the mutual consent of the parties hereto in perfecting and executing the plans and in obtaining the right to run the cars of the parties hereto across said Bridge and all future expenses of every kind in connection with the perfection and execution of the plans and the carrying out of the details thereof, including the entire cost of all changes in existing tracks which may be necessary to make connections with the Bridge property, and all necessary work, including materials therefor, upon the property of The New York and Brooklyn Bridge, shall be borne and paid by the parties hereto in the proportion and percentages hereinafter specified.

The use by any one party hereto of the tracks or property of any other party hereto for the purpose of operating its cars across said Bridge, and the manner of making connections therefor, the extent of such use and the compensation for such use and the expense of connections, if not agreed upon by such parties, shall be fixed by arbitration in the usual manner by disinterested arbitrators. But neither one of the parties of the second, third or fourth part hereto shall have the right by virtue of this agreement to run its cars over the tracks of the parties of the first part, except on Fulton street between Prospect street and Smith street; on Sands street between Fulton street and Jay street; on Navy street between De Kalb avenue and Park avenue; on Park avenue between Navy street and Raymond street; on the lot on the northeast corner of Sands street and Fulton street, and on Liberty street, where the tracks are constructed thereon. Neither one of the parties of the first, third or fourth part hereto shall have the right by virtue of this agreement to run its cars over the tracks of the party of the second part except on Adams street between Fulton street and Prospect street; on Concord street between Washington street and Navy street; on Navy street between Concord street and Park avenue, and on Park avenue between Navy and Raymond streets. Neither one of the parties of the first, second or fourth parts hereto shall have the right by virtue of this agreement to run its cars over the tracks of the party of the third part except on Washington street between Fulton street and Prospect street. Neither one of the parties of the first, second or third part hereto shall have the right by virtue of this agreement to run its cars over the tracks of the party of the fourth part except on Jay street between Fulton street and Prospect street; on Prospect street between Fulton street and Jay street, and on High street between Washington street and Jay street. If any party hereto shall at any time cease to operate its cars across said Bridge, then its rights to operate its cars over the tracks of any other party hereto under or by virtue of this agreement shall thereupon cease and terminate.

Should anyone of the parties hereto refuse to execute or to enter into any contracts which may be necessary for the performance of the work herein required, or refuse to pay its portion of the liability therefor incurred as herein provided, such party shall forfeit all rights under this contract and also the further right to operate its cars over said Bridge, without affecting any other remedy for such liability.

Any assessment or charge made by the said Bridge Trustees or by either of the Cities of New York or Brooklyn for the privilege of operating the cars of the parties hereto over the Bridge shall be borne and paid for in like manner and proportion except specific charges per car or per passenger, which shall be borne by the parties hereto severally.

The parties hereto shall share in the use of the tracks, equipments and terminals to be placed on said Bridge as aforesaid in the following proportion, that is to say, in the number of cars to be run on such tracks; parties of the first part shall be entitled to sixty per cent. (60 per cent.), the party of the second part shall be entitled to twenty-four per cent. (24 per cent.), the party of the third part shall be entitled to ten per cent. (10 per cent.), the party of the fourth part shall be entitled to six per cent. (6 per cent.). The number of cars of each of the parties hereto upon the Bridge during any one hour shall be distributed in the same proportion as nearly as practicable, but if any party hereto shall not operate upon the Bridge at any one hour the maximum number of cars it is entitled to, no other party hereto shall, by reason thereof, be required to reduce the maximum number of cars it is entitled to operate upon said Bridge at the same time; nor shall the percentage of the expenditures to be paid by any party be affected thereby.

The Superintendent of Terminals hereinafter provided for shall prescribe from time to time, and may prescribe for such particular times as he may deem desirable, the total number of cars that shall be operated by all the parties hereto during the several hours of the day respectively, or during any hour or series of hours, and each party hereto shall then during each such hour be limited to its proportion of such total number of cars to each such hour, and the Superintendent of Terminals shall fix and promulgate the time tables for each such hour accordingly, so as to distribute each party's proportion of cars through such hour as equally as may be practicable.

Should any party hereto during any one hour operate upon said Bridge a greater number of cars than its due proportion as herein specified, then such party shall pay to the other parties hereto as liquidated damages, and not as a penalty, Ten Dollars ($10) for each car in excess of its proper proportionate share as aforesaid, the amounts so paid or collected to be distributed between the other parties in the proportions above specified, and such other parties may sue jointly for the whole amount thereof or severally for their respective amounts therefor. Such payment shall be additional to any other remedy for such violation and shall not affect or impair any other remedy by injunction or otherwise.

In the operation of the various lines of cars over the Bridge, they shall be under the sole charge and direction of a joint employee to be appointed by the parties hereto, each party being entitled to vote upon such appointment in the proportion above specified, such joint employee to be known as "Superintendent of Terminals," and he shall be removed on written demand of any party hereto served upon all the other parties. While entering upon the property of the Bridge on the Brooklyn side, while upon said Bridge and until and while leaving the Bridge property, all cars of or operated by any or all of the parties hereto shall be under the direction and control of said Superintendent, and all employees of the parties hereto shall act in strict accordance with his orders, and conform to all rules and regulations that may be adopted by the parties hereto or by said Superintendent not inconsistent therewith; subject, however, to the control of the said Bridge Trustees.

Each party hereto may bid for the furnishing of the electrical or other power necessary to operate the cars over the Bridge for a period of five years, at a rate per trip, which may include cars operated during the summer without electric heaters, and a separate or higher rate for cars operated with electric heaters; and the party hereto agreeing to furnish power at the lowest price shall be entitled to do so. Each party hereto on or before the fifth day of each month shall make a statement to the party furnishing such power of the number of cars which it has operated over said Bridge during the month immediately preceding, which statement shall be verified by the Superintendent of Terminals, and compensation for such power and heat shall be paid on or before the tenth of each month to the party furnishing the power at the agreed or bid rate per round trip.

All expense of repairs and maintenance, of tracks, roadways and terminals, including the operation of the terminal in New York, which may be required to be made by the parties hereto, and all other expenses of every nature and description in connection with the operation of the cars of the parties hereto, shall be adjusted in the proportion herein specified, and bills therefor, properly certified by said Superintendent of Terminals, shall be presented to each party hereto on or before the fifth of each month for the next preceding month, and shall be paid on or before the tenth of the next month.

Each party hereto shall be responsible for all damages from accidents or injuries, caused by the negligence of its own employees, whether such damage be to the cars or property of any of the other parties hereto, or to any passenger in or upon any of said cars, or to any vehicle or person while upon said Bridge, it being the intent of this agreement that all liability incurred by any party hereto from the negligence of its own employees, or defects in its cars or equipment, shall be borne solely and wholly by such party; and that all liability from joint operation, as from negligence of joint employees or defective apparatus, elevators, tracks, platforms, or overhead work furnished or used jointly by the parties hereto, shall be borne jointly by the parties hereto in the proportion above stated.

The proportions mentioned herein for apportioning the expenditures between the parties hereto, including the preliminary expense of preparing and securing plans and rights of way as well as the work of erecting, completing, maintenance, operation and repair of all equipment and overhead work on said Bridge shall be as follows: parties of the first part, sixty per cent. (60 per cent.), party of the second part, twenty-four per cent. (24 per cent.), party of the third part, ten per cent (10 per cent.), party of the fourth part, six per cent. (6 per cent.).

The corporation proposed to be organized by Tom L. Johnson for the purpose of becoming the owner of the railroads and franchises now operated by the Nassau Electric Railroad Company from Fulton Ferry to Evergreen Cemetery, known as the Park Avenue and Central Avenue route, shall, on becoming such owner, be deemed jointly with the Nassau Electric Railroad Company to constitute the party of the second part hereto.

In Witness Whereof, the parties hereto have caused this agreement to be duly executed the day and year first written.

THE BROOKLYN HEIGHTS RAILROAD COMPANY,

[SEAL.] By C. L. ROSSITER,
President.

Attest:
T. S. WILLIAMS,
Secretary.

THE BROOKLYN, QUEENS COUNTY AND SUBURBAN RAILROAD COMPANY,

[SEAL.] By C. L. ROSSITER,
President.

Attest:
T. S. WILLIAMS,
Secretary.

NASSAU ELECTRIC RAILROAD COMPANY,

[SEAL.] By A. L. JOHNSON,
President.

Attest:
W. F. HAM,
Secretary.

TOM L. JOHNSON.

THE BROOKLYN CITY AND NEWTOWN RAILROAD COMPANY,

[SEAL.] By JOHN N. PARTRIDGE,
President.

Attest:
DUNCAN B. CANNON,
Secretary.

THE CONEY ISLAND AND BROOKLYN RAILROAD COMPANY,

[SEAL.] By D. W. SULLIVAN,
President.

Attest:
WILLIS BROWER,
Secretary.

STATE OF NEW YORK,
  County of Kings,   } *ss.:*
  City of Brooklyn,

On this 29th day of September, in the year 1897, before me personally came Albert L. Johnson and William F. Ham, to me known, who, being by me severally duly sworn, each for himself did depose and say: That the said Albert L. Johnson resided in the City of New York, and the said William F. Ham resided in the City of Brooklyn, that the said Albert L. Johnson is the President and the said William F. Ham is the Secretary of the Nassau Electric Railroad Company, the corporation described in and which executed the above instrument; that he knew the seal of said corporation; that the seal affixed to said instrument was such corporate seal, that it was so affixed by order of the Board of Directors of such corporation, and that he signed his name thereto by like order.

A. L. BROUGHAM,
Commissioner of Deeds,
City of Brooklyn.

STATE OF NEW YORK,
  County of Kings,   } *ss.:*
  City of Brooklyn,

On this 29th day of September, in the year 1897, before me personally came John L. Heins and Duncan B. Cannon, to me known, who, being by me severally duly sworn, each for himself did depose and say: That the said John L. Heins resided in the City of Brooklyn, and the said Duncan B. Cannon resided in the City of New York; that the said John L. Heins is the President and the said Duncan B. Cannon is the Secretary of The Brooklyn City and Newtown Railroad Company, the corporation described in and which executed the above instrument; that he knew the seal of said corporation; that the seal affixed to said instrument was such corporate seal; that it was so affixed by order of the Board of Directors of such corporation and that he signed his name thereto by like order.

A. L. BROUGHAM,
Commissioner of Deeds,
City of Brooklyn.

STATE OF NEW YORK,
  County of Kings,   } ss.:
  City of Brooklyn,

On this 29th day of September, in the year 1897, before me personally came D. W. Sullivan and Willis Brower to me known, who, being by me severally duly sworn, each for himself did depose and say: That he resided in the City of Brooklyn, that the said D. W. Sullivan is the President and the said Willis Brower is the Secretary of The Coney Island and Brooklyn Railroad Company, the corporation described in and which executed the above instrument; that he knew the seal of said corporation; that the seal affixed to said instrument was such corporate seal; that it was so affixed by order of the Board of Directors of such corporation and that he signed his name thereto by like order.

                A. L. BROUGHAM,
                      Commissioner of Deeds,
                            City of Brooklyn.

STATE OF NEW YORK,
  County of Kings,   } ss.:
  City of Brooklyn,

On this 15th day of October, in the year 1897, before me personally appeared Tom L. Johnson, to me known to be one of persons described in and who executed the above instrument, and he duly acknowledged to me that he executed the same.

                V. W. WICKES,
                      Notary Public,
                          Kings County.

STATE OF NEW YORK,⎫
  County of Kings,   ⎬ ss.:
  City of Brooklyn,   ⎭

On this 24th day of August, in the year 1897, before me personally came D. W. Sullivan and Willis Brower, to me known, who being by me severally duly sworn, each for himself did depose and say: That he resided in the City of Brooklyn, that the said D. W. Sullivan is the President and the said Willis Brower is the Secretary of The Coney Island and Brooklyn Railroad Company, the corporation described in and which executed the above instrument; that he knew the seal of said corporation; that the seal affixed to said instrument was such corporate seal; that it was so affixed by order of the Board of Directors of such corporation and that he signed his name thereto by like order.

V. W. WICKES,
Notary Public.

STATE OF NEW YORK,⎫
  County of Kings,   ⎬ ss.:
  City of Brooklyn,   ⎭

On this 24th day of August, in the year 1897, before me personally appeared Tom L. Johnson, to me known to be one of the persons described in and who executed the above instrument, and he duly acknowledged to me that he executed the same.

V. W. WICKES,
Notary Public.

SUPPLEMENTARY AGREEMENT
ASSOCIATED TROLLEY COMPANIES
September 29, 1897.

SUPPLEMENTARY AGREEMENT, made this 29th day of September, 1897, between THE BROOKLYN HEIGHTS RAILROAD COMPANY and THE BROOKLYN, QUEENS COUNTY AND SUBURBAN RAILROAD COMPANY, parties of the first part; NASSAU ELECTRIC RAILROAD COMPANY, party of the second part; THE BROOKLYN CITY AND NEWTOWN RAILROAD COMPANY, party of the third part; and THE CONEY ISLAND AND BROOKLYN RAILROAD COMPANY, party of the fourth part, WITNESSETH:

WHEREAS, the parties hereto entered into an agreement with each other bearing date August 23d, 1897, in relation to crossing the New York and Brooklyn Bridge in pursuance of contracts between the Trustees of the New York and Brooklyn Bridge, and each of the several parties hereto, except The Brooklyn, Queens County and Suburban Railroad Company, bearing date August 23d, 1897, and

WHEREAS, said last-mentioned contracts have been modified by supplementary contracts bearing date September 29th, 1897, between the Trustees of the New York and Brooklyn Bridge, and each of the parties hereto, except The Brooklyn, Queens County and Suburban Railroad Company,

Now, THEREFORE, this Supplementary Agreement witnesseth, that the first above-mentioned contract between the parties hereto bearing date August 23d, 1897, shall continue in full force and effect, except as its provisions are necessarily modified by the fact of the execution and delivery of the last above-mentioned supplementary contracts; and the plans attached to the last above-mentioned contracts, and the provisions of the last above-mentioned contracts relating to crossing said Bridge shall be deemed to be the plans and provisions for crossing said Bridge referred to in the first above-mentioned contract.

The corporation proposed to be organized by Tom L. Johnson for the purpose of becoming the owner of the railroads and franchises now operated by the Nassau Electric Railroad

Company from Fulton Ferry to Evergreen Cemetery, known as the Park Avenue and Central Avenue route, shall, on becoming such owner, be deemed jointly with the Nassau Electric Railroad Company to constitute the party of the second part hereto.

IN WITNESS WHEREOF, the parties hereto have caused this agreement to be duly executed the day and the year first above written.

THE BROOKLYN HEIGHTS RAILROAD COMPANY,
[SEAL.] By C. L. ROSSITER,
President.

Attest:
  T. S. WILLIAMS,
    Secretary,

THE BROOKLYN, QUEENS COUNTY AND SUBURBAN RAILROAD COMPANY,
[SEAL.] By C. L. ROSSITER,
President.

Attest:
  T. S. WILLIAMS,
    Secretary.

NASSAU ELECTRIC RAILROAD COMPANY,
[SEAL.] By A. L. JOHNSON,
President.

Attest:
  W. F. HAM,
    Secretary.

TOM L. JOHNSON.

THE BROOKLYN CITY AND NEWTOWN RAILROAD COMPANY,
[SEAL.] By JOHN L. HEINS,
President.

Attest:
  DUNCAN B. CANNON,
    Secretary.

THE CONEY ISLAND AND BROOKLYN RAILROAD COMPANY,
[SEAL.] By D. W. SULLIVAN,
President.

Attest:
  WILLIS BROWER,
    Notary Public.

STATE OF NEW YORK, }
  County of Kings, } *ss.:*
  City of Brooklyn, }

On this 29th day of September, in the year 1897, before me personally came Clinton L. Rossiter and Timothy S. Williams, to me known, who, being by me severally duly sworn, each for himself did depose and say: That he resided in the City of Brooklyn, that the said Clinton L. Rossiter is the President and the said Timothy S. Williams is the Secretary of the Brooklyn Heights Railroad Company, the corporation described in and which executed the above instrument; that he knew the seal of said corporation; that the seal affixed to said instrument was such corporate seal, that it was so affixed by order of the Board of Directors of such corporation and that he signed his name thereto by like order.

                A. L. BROUGHAM,
                    Commissioner of Deeds.
                        City of Brooklyn.

STATE OF NEW YORK, }
  County of Kings, } *ss.:*
  City of Brooklyn, }

On this 29th day of September, in the year 1897, before me personally came Clinton L. Rossiter and Timothy S. Williams, to me known, who, being by me severally duly sworn, each for himself did depose and say: That he resided in the City of Brooklyn, that the said Clinton L. Rossiter is the President and the said Timothy S. Williams is the Secretary of the Brooklyn, Queens County and Suburban Railroad Company, the corporation described in and which executed the above instrument; that he knew the seal of said corporation; that the seal affixed to said instrument was such corporate seal; that it was so affixed by order of the Board of Directors of such corporation, and that he signed his name thereto by like order.

                A. L. BROUGHAM,
                    Commissioner of Deeds,
                        City of Brooklyn.

STATE OF NEW YORK,
County of Kings, } *ss.:*
City of Brooklyn,

On this 24th day of August, in the year 1897, before me personally came Clinton L. Rossiter and Timothy S. Williams, to me known, who, being by me severally duly sworn, each for himself did depose and say: That he resided in the City of Brooklyn; that the said Clinton L. Rossiter is the President and the said Timothy S. Williams is the Secretary of The Brooklyn Heights Railroad Company, the corporation described in and which executed the above instrument; that he knew the seal of said corporation; that the seal affixed to the said instrument was such corporate seal; that it was so affixed by order of the Board of Directors of such corporation, and that he signed his name thereto by like order.

V. W. WICKES,
Notary Public.

STATE OF NEW YORK,
County of Kings, } *ss.:*
City of Brooklyn,

On this 24th day of August, in the year 1897, before me personally came Clinton L. Rossiter and Timothy S. Williams, to me known, who, being by me severally duly sworn, each for himself, did depose and say: That he resided in the City of Brooklyn; that the said Clinton L. Rossiter is the President and the said Timothy S. Williams is the Secretary of The Brooklyn, Queens County and Suburban Railroad Company, the corporation described in and which executed the above instrument; that he knew the seal of said corporation; that the seal affixed to said instrument was such corporate seal; that it was so affixed by order of the Board of Directors of such corporation, and that he signed his name thereto by like order.

V. W. WICKES,
Notary Public.

STATE OF NEW YORK,⎫
  County of Kings, ⎬ *ss.:*
  City of Brooklyn, ⎭

On this 24th day of August, in the year 1897, before me personally came Albert L. Johnson and William F. Ham, to me known, who being by me severally duly sworn, each for himself, did depose and say: That he resided in the City of Brooklyn, that the said Albert L. Johnson is the President and the said William F. Ham is the Secretary of the Nassau Electric Railroad Company, the corporation described in and which executed the above instrument; that he knew the seal of said corporation; that the seal affixed to said instrument was such corporate seal, that it was so affixed by order of the Board of Directors of such corporation, and that he signed his name thereto by like order.

                        V. W. WICKES,
                            Notary Public.

STATE OF NEW YORK,⎫
  County of Kings, ⎬ *ss.:*
  City of Brooklyn, ⎭

On this 24th day of August, in the year 1897, before me personally came John N. Partridge and Duncan B. Cannon, to me known, who being by me severally duly sworn, each for himself, did depose and say: That he resided in the City of Brooklyn, that the said John N. Partridge is the President and the said Duncan B. Cannon is the Secretary of The Brooklyn City and Newtown Railroad Company, the corporation described in and which executed the above instrument; that he knew the seal of said corporation; that the seal affixed to said instrument was such corporate seal; that it was so affixed by order of the Board of Directors of such corporation, and that he signed his name thereto by like order.

                        V. W. WICKES,
                            Notary Public.

AGREEMENT (ORIGINAL).

BROOKLYN ELEVATED RAILROAD COMPANY.

THIS AGREEMENT, made this 23d day of August, 1897, between THE TRUSTEES OF THE NEW YORK AND BROOKLYN BRIDGE, party of the first part, and THE BROOKLYN ELEVATED RAILROAD COMPANY, party of the second part, WITNESSETH:

That the party of the first part, for and in consideration of the payments to be made to it by the party of the second part, and of the faithful, just and full performance of the undertakings, covenants and agreements to be by said party of the second part performed and carried out as hereinafter set forth, doth, subject to the conditions and restrictions herein provided and expressed, grant and lease to the party of the second part the right and privilege to enter upon the premises of the party of the first part with its cars, for the transportation of passengers, and to have the cars of said party of the second part, and the passengers using and traveling in said cars transported and operated by the party of the first part across its Bridge, and to that end to cross, intersect, join and unite its railroad with the railroad operated by the party of the first part upon and across the New York and Brooklyn Bridge, subject, however, in all things in such crossing, intersecting, joining and uniting to the control and direction of the Chief Engineer of the party of the first part; the terms upon which this lease, license, privilege or grant is made, the conditions subject to which the rights hereby conferred upon the party of the second part are to be exercised, and the covenants by said party of the second part to be observed and performed, are as follows, to wit:

I.—The said Railroad Company shall arrange for the connection of its tracks with the tracks of the New York and Brooklyn Bridge at some point at or north of Tillary street, in the City of Brooklyn, to be determined upon by the Chief Engineer of the party of the first part and convenient for that purpose, so that the trains of said Company shall approach and enter the property of the said Trustees upon a single track, which shall be connected

with the north tracks now owned and controlled by the said
Trustees over said Bridge, and so that the trains of said Company on returning from New York shall leave the property of
the said Trustees upon a single track, which shall be connected
with the south tracks now owned and controlled by said Trustees,
over said Bridge, in such manner as may be designated by the
Chief Engineer of said Bridge.

The said Trustees shall permit the said Railroad Company to
construct a platform or platforms and stairs between the "tail
tracks" of said Bridge at the New York terminal thereof, for the
use of said Railroad Company and its passengers, subject, however, to the control and the use of the same by the said Trustees,
and to the use thereof by any subsequent lessees to whom said
Trustees may grant the right to use the same, provided that in
the event of such right being extended the lessee thereof shall
be required to pay to the Brooklyn Elevated Railroad Company
such proportion of the cost of construction of said platform and
stairways as shall be determined by said Trustees.

Said Railroad Company shall prepare the plans for such connections, platforms and stairways, and do and pay for the work,
provided only that said plans shall be approved by the Chief
Engineer of the party of the first part and the work carried on
subject to his approval and inspection, and such plans are those
hereto attached, which it is hereby covenanted are and constitute
a part of this agreement.

II.—The location of the said tracks and of the curves and
switches necessary to connect the present tracks of the said railroad with the tracks of the said Bridge, and all the constructions
of every kind necessary to the use of the said tracks, as herein
provided, shall be under the absolute control and direction of the
Chief Engineer of the said Bridge, and no construction of any
kind connected therewith or relating thereto shall be had or used
unless the plan or plans therefor have been first submitted to the
said Engineer, and have been approved by him and are hereto
attached as aforesaid.

III.—The expense of all changes necessary in the construction
upon the said Bridge or the approach thereto in order to permit
the delivery of the cars of the said Elevated Railroad Company
to the control of the said Trustees of the Bridge, and to permit

the transportation thereof and return thereof to said Railroad Company, and the maintenance and repairing of all changes and additions aforesaid shall be borne and paid for by the said Railroad Company. Provided, that the cost of whatever part of such construction which shall be used by more than one railroad company, or the necessity for the creation of which shall be common to the bringing upon the Bridge of cars of more than one railroad company, shall be borne by the several railroad companies in such shares and proportions as they may agree upon, or, if they fail to agree, in such shares and proportions as the Trustees of the said Bridge may determine.

All plans and contracts for labor and material necessary to the construction aforesaid of the approaches to the premises of the Trustees, and to the entry upon and departure from said premises by said Railroad Company, shall be made by said Railroad Company in its own name and upon its own responsibility; all material necessary to be used upon the premises of the Trustees shall be supplied by said Railroad Company, and all labor to be performed upon said premises shall be performed by said Railroad Company and the cost thereof paid by said Railroad Company before entering said premises with its cars. All of such work and material shall be subject to approval and rejection by the said Trustees; all of such constructions upon property belonging to the Trustees of the New York and Brooklyn Bridge shall become and be the property of the said The Trustees of the New York and Brooklyn Bridge, when and as soon as work shall be begun or material necessary to such construction shall be delivered upon premises of said party of the first part; all work done in pursuance of the terms of this contract by said Railroad Company shall be so carried on as in no manner to interfere with, limit or obstruct the operation of the railroad of and belonging to said Trustees upon and over said Bridge.

IV.—All rights of way, franchises and property necessary to be secured in order to construct the tracks upon which to enter upon and leave the said Bridge property shall be secured and paid for by the said Railroad Company.

V.—Each car, except motor cars, of the said Elevated Railroad Company, intended to be used upon the railroad of the Bridge, shall be equipped with grips in form and construction as may be designated by the Chief Engineer of the Bridge, together with the same appliances for braking while on the Bridge, as employed upon the cars of the Trustees of the Bridge, or as directed by said Chief Engineer. One car on each train shall also be equipped with electric motors on each truck identical with those adopted by the Bridge Trustees, or as may be suggested and approved by the Chief Engineer of the Bridge, for the purpose of switching trains at termini. All elevated railroad cars sent or used upon the Bridge shall have side doors, in form and construction to be approved by said Chief Engineer.

VI.—All cars used on the Bridge service and all equipment and appliances relating thereto, located on Bridge property, shall be subject at all times to inspection by the Bridge authorities, who shall have power to forbid rights on the Bridge to cars that may, for any reason, be unsatisfactory, and to direct the removal of any old or inadequate equipment or appliances, and the substitution therefor of others of approved character. On arriving at the place nearest to the point where the cars of said Railroad Company shall enter upon the premises of the Trustees of the Bridge, as the same shall be fixed and located by the said Bridge Trustees, the locomotives shall be detached from the trains upon the said elevated railroad, and such trains shall then be propelled by the electric motor cars, already referred to, over such tracks as the Trustees of the said Bridge shall designate, to the point at which the cable is lifted into grips, from which point the train shall proceed over the Bridge by cable traction, precisely as the cars of the Bridge Railway are now operated; and on returning from New York the said trains, after passing the unloading platforms at the Brooklyn terminal of the said Bridge, shall be propelled by the electric motor car as aforesaid, to the place upon the track of the said elevated railroad company selected by the Chief Engineer of the party of the first part. From the time when the trains of the said Railroad Company enter upon the premises of said Trustees until, on the return of the trains from New York, they shall depart from said premises, said cars and trains shall be under the exclusive management and control of the Trustees of the New York and Brooklyn Bridge and of their employees.

VII.—The said Trustees shall have full and complete power to make and adopt all other rules and regulations which to them shall seem reasonable and proper, relating to the transporting of the cars of the said Railroad Company over the said Bridge, including the method of payment of tolls, the style of cars to be used and the condition of the cars, the switching of cars and the use of platforms, and to amend or alter any of such rules or regulations so as to secure the safety and comfort of persons using the said Bridge, and to subserve the purpose for which said Bridge was constructed.

But the Railroad Company shall be allowed to place and retain advertising signs inside its cars.

The Railroad Company shall not bring upon the premises of the party of the first part or deliver to them for transportation across the Bridge, any cars in which smoking shall be permitted, while the cars of the said Railroad Company are upon the premises of the party of the first part.

VIII.—The said Railroad Company shall pay to the said Trustees of the New York and Brooklyn Bridge the sum of twelve and one-half cents per round trip for each car transported as aforesaid, provided that if at any time the regulations adopted by the said Trustees shall be altered or modified so as to permit the said Railroad Company to operate cars across said Bridge by their own power, the said Railroad Company shall pay the sum of five cents per round trip for each car so operated; provided that, pursuant to the provisions of chapter 663 Laws of 1897, the said party of the second part shall not, by reason of the payments by it to be made to the party of the first part as herein provided, or otherwise, or for any reason whatever, " charge any fare in excess of, or additional to, the fare exacted by it from any passenger for one continuous ride upon any of its routes in either of the cities of New York or Brooklyn, as the case may be, so that the said route of said Corporation operated across said Bridge hereunder, so far as the exaction of a fare is concerned, shall be taken and deemed to be a part of the continuous route, or one of the continuous routes, of the said Railroad Corporation whereon one fare is exacted, so that no extra or additional fare shall be exacted by said party of the second part from any passenger carried to or from the Bridge and across the Bridge in addition to the fare exacted from such passenger for carriage to and from the Bridge only."

IX.—All trains coming upon the premises of the party of the first part, shall, when approaching an intersection with any track of said party of the first part, be brought to a full stop before crossing the same, and shall not be again started until signal to proceed be given by a man employed for such purpose by said party of the first part.

X.—The said Railroad Company shall protect and hold harmless the said Trustees from and against all losses, damages and claims for damages, actions, recoveries, costs, disbursements and expenses of every nature arising from, based upon, connected with, or in any manner charged to be due to injury to person or property received or sustained by any person upon and in the cars of the said Company whenever and wherever upon the premises of said Trustees such injuries may arise, be received or sustained, or which may be caused by the cars of the said Railroad Company, or which may arise from or be connected with the presence and operation of such cars upon such premises or which shall in any wise be connected with or arise out of the bringing of the said cars upon the premises of the party of the first part, or transporting or operating them upon, over or across the same, or which may arise from or be connected with the making, building, constructing, erecting or changing of any work, of every kind necessary for the bringing of the cars of the party of the second part upon the said Bridge and the operating and the transporting of the same across the said Bridge, or in any and every wise growing out of the use of the said Bridge and any of the premises, appurtenances and appliances thereunto belonging by the party of the second part.

And the said Railroad Company shall further protect and hold harmless the said Trustees from and against losses, damages, and claims for damages, actions, recoveries, costs, disbursements and expenses of every nature which may arise or result from any failure or delay on the part of the said Railroad Company to promptly and regularly operate and transport its cars across said Bridge in either direction, or for any delay or hindrance to said cars while in transit, from whatever cause or reason such neglect or refusal or delay may arise, or which may arise to any person using the said Bridge in any way or manner who shall be injured in person or property, or hindered or delayed in the use of said Bridge by reason of any matter, thing or occurrence arising from or connected with the operation of the cars across the said structure. And should there at any time occur a block upon the roadway of said Bridge, or interference with the use of said roadway by the public by reason of the operation of the cars of the said Railroad Company across the Bridge, the said Railroad Company shall protect and hold harmless the said Trustees from and against all claims or damages resulting from the same. And should there be caused by the operation of the said cars, or in any way connected therewith, any accident upon such roadway, the said Railroad Company shall in like manner protect and hold harmless the said Trustees against losses, damages, and claims for damages, actions, recoveries, costs, disbursements and expenses of every nature, which may arise therefrom.

And the said Railroad Company shall further protect and hold harmless said Trustees from and against any and all suits, lets, hindrances, actions, recoveries, claims, damages, costs, disbursements and expenses of every kind, nature, amount and description, which may arise, be made and presented, brought, instituted, sustained or recovered on the ground of deprivation of owners of property adjoining premises of the party of the first part of light, or air, or interruption of either or of damages of any and every nature consequent upon and resulting from the bringing of the cars of said Railroad upon premises of party of the first part and operating the same thereupon, and over said premises and Bridge.

But nothing herein is to be construed as rendering the party of the second part liable to the Trustees or to any person, firm or corporation for any damage, injury or hindrance, or render it liable to suffer any recovery against it by said Trustees for any delay or accident arising solely from faulty construction or imperfect track or appurtenances of or connected with the Bridge, or solely from negligence on the part of the agents or servants of the Trustees.

XI.—The supervision, management and control of cars of the Railroad Company shall in every particular and at all times be wholly exercised by the Trustees of the New York and Brooklyn Bridge within the discretion and at the dictation of the Chief Engineer of said Trustees from the delivery of said cars upon the premises of the Trustees till their departure therefrom, provided only that while said Chief Engineer shall at all times regulate and limit in his discretion the number of cars of the Railroad Company which may be operated as aforesaid, nevertheless, inasmuch as it is in contemplation by the parties hereto that privileges similar to those herein set forth are to be granted to the Kings County Elevated Railway Company, the number of cars of the Brooklyn Elevated Railroad Company to be operated upon and over said Bridge shall not be limited to less tran two cars of the Brooklyn Elevated Railroad Company to one car of the Kings County Elevated Railway Company.

It is hereby mutually covenanted and agreed that no delay, hindrance or refusal to receive and operate cars of the Brooklyn Elevated Railroad Company shall be made or exercised by reason of failure for any reason on the part of the Kings County Elevated Railway Company to deliver the quota of cars upon the premises of the Trustees regularly and promptly, in accordance with any schedule or rule of operation which may be promulgated by said Chief Engineer.

And whereas, the exercise of the right to cause its cars to be operated across the Bridge necessitates the surrender by the Trustees to such use of one set of tracks for such purpose, thereby reducing the number of Bridge trains which it is possible for said Trustees to operate; now, therefore, it is hereby mutually agreed that the number of trains and cars to be delivered by said Railroad Company to said Trustees shall at all times equal one-half the number of trains and cars belonging to said Trustees and operated by them, at the date of the execution of these presents, provided only that should the Kings County Elevated Railway secure from said Trustees provisions similar to those hereby granted, the said party of the second part may reduce the number of cars to be delivered by it to not less than one-third the number operated by said Trustees at the date of the execution of these presents.

XII.—The term of the right and privilege hereby granted to the party of the second part to enter upon the premises of the party of the first part with its cars for the transportation of passengers, and to have its cars and the passengers using and traveling in the same, transported and operated by the said Trustees across its Bridge, and to that end to cross, intersect, join and unite its railroad with the railroad operated by the party of the first part, shall be terminable at the option of either party hereto after the expiration of ten years from the date when this contract shall be duly executed, provided only, that if in the opinion of the party of the first part, or its legal successors, and of the Mayor of the City of New York, and of the President of the Borough of Brooklyn, to be hereafter elected pursuant to the provisions of chapter 378 of the Laws of 1897, or in the opinion of the majority of them, it should be determined that it is against the public interest to continue the operation of the trains, or cars, of the party of the second part, upon, over and across the Bridge, or if the said party of the second part should for itself determine that the facilities afforded it are inadequate for its passenger service, then, and in that event, this agreement and all of the rights and privileges granted to said party of the second part, and obligations assumed by it, shall be terminable on and after three months' notice, in writing, by either party to the other that it elects to determine said contract.

XIII.—The said Railroad Company before entering in any manner upon the premises of the party of the first part for the performance of any work necessary to make the connections hereinbefore provided for shall execute and deliver to the Trustees of said Bridge its bond in the sum of Fifty Thousand Dollars, and in such form and with such securities as the said Trustees shall prescribe (which bond shall be approved as to form and manner of execution and sufficiency of sureties by the Counsel to said Trustees) conditioned that the said Company shall promptly complete the work entered upon by it as hereinbefore provided, and if it shall fail so to do, that it shall pay to said Trustees of said Bridge the necessary expenses of completing the same or of removing any portions of said structures which are upon the property of the said the Trustees of the Bridge, and of restoring the Bridge and all the premises of the party of the first part, and all things appurtenant thereto, to the present condition, whichever the said Trustees shall elect to do; and further conditioned that the said Railroad Company shall observe, obey and keep each and every rule and regulation made and adopted by the said Trustees as hereinbefore provided, and for the discharge of any and all liability hereby imposed and which may arise or be incurred pursuant to the provisions of this contract, and further conditioned that the said Railroad Company shall and will faithfully, promptly and fully pay to said Trustees the rental hereby reserved and the charges hereby imposed.

And for a failure and neglect to observe, obey and keep such rules and regulations, or any of them, and for a failure to promptly make payment to said Trustees of the rental reserved and charges by this agreement imposed, the said Trustees may revoke the said agreement so far as it affects the said Railroad Company, and thereupon said Railroad Company shall forfeit all rights and privileges heretofore enjoyed thereunder.

XIV.—It is hereby covenanted, agreed and understood that the foregoing agreement in all its parts does and is intended to apply to the Brooklyn Elevated Railroad Company, and to any and all companies which, as the result of the reorganization of said Company, now pending may be and become the legal successor to said company and owner of its rights, privileges, and franchises, and to Frederick Uhlmann, Esq., as Receiver of the corporate rights, franchises and properties of said Brooklyn Elevated Railroad Company, and to any and all successors in office of said Frederick Uhlmann, as Receiver, and that in order to be effectual and binding this instrument shall be executed by the officers of said Railroad Company and by said Receiver.

It is further covenanted that said Receiver shall, before executing this agreement, obtain the consent of the Supreme Court, having control and jurisdiction of and over the acts of such Receiver to the execution thereof.

XV.—The said Railroad Company doth hereby further covenant, promise and agree that for and in consideration of the provisions of this instrument and of the privileges and grants thereby extended to it by the party of the first part, it will commence the work preparatory to the exercise of the privileges hereby extended within sixty days after the date of the execution of this instrument, and that all of the said work hereinbefore provided for as necessary to the operation of the cars of the said Railroad Company over the Bridge shall be fully completed, and said operation of cars be regularly commenced within ten months after the date of the execution of these premises, provided only, that should either the commencement, continuation or finishing of such work or the operation of the cars of the said Railroad Company upon, over and across the premises of the party of the first part be delayed by litigation, strikes, or causes of delay not created by the party of the second part and not to be avoided by ordinary precautions on its part, the time necessarily consumed in such litigation and by such strikes, or causes of delay aforesaid, shall be added to the time herein provided for the beginning and completion of the work aforesaid, and further provided that for failure to comply with this provision of this agreement, or by reason of the institution by or at the instigation of the said Railroad Company of litigation of any nature, instituted in any wise for the purpose of increasing the time within which the provisions of this contract shall be put in effect, the said party of the first part may, at the discretion of said Trustees, revoke each and every privilege hereinbefore contained and set forth, and upon such revocation all work and material put upon the premises of the party of the first part by the said Railroad Company shall be and become forfeit to the said Trustees without damage or compensation therefor to the said Railroad Company.

It is hereby covenanted and agreed that the said Railroad Company shall not in any way enter upon the premises of the party of the first part or commence any work or construction thereon, nor place any material to be used in such work and construction upon the premises of the party of the first part until all the work and construction to be undertaken and performed by the party of the second part outside of the property of the said Trustees, and necessary and sufficient for the purpose of making the connection between the railroad of the said party of the second part, and that of the said Trustees, as hereinbefore provided, shall be fairly under way, to the end that all construction necessary to cross the Bridge by cars of the aforesaid railroad may be completed at about the same time; nor shall said Railroad Company enter upon or do any work of construction upon the premises of said Trustees until it shall have secured its right of way and removed any and every injunction that may have been granted by a court of competent jurisdiction.

And also that the said Railroad Company shall not in any way interfere with the operation of the railroad operated by the Trustees, pending construction necessary to connect the railroad of the party of the second part with the Bridge and permit its cars to be operated thereon, nor shall said Railroad Company use the structure of the Bridge for the storage of material to be used in such work and construction, nor permit its employees or the employees of contractors to use the Bridge premises as a rendezvous or resting place, but work of construction is to proceed day by day without interruption, except if the Railroad Company is enjoined from proceeding by the court, or in the event of strikes or hindrance or delays beyond the control of the Railroad Company, and it is expressly stipulated that in all matters connected with construction and work on the premises of the Trustees that the Chief Engineer of the Bridge shall have absolute supervision and control.

IN WITNESS WHEREOF, on this 23d day of August, eighteen hundred and ninety-seven, the party of the first part, The Trustees of the New York and Brooklyn Bridge, has caused these presents to be subscribed by its President and its corporate seal to be hereto affixed, and on the same day the said Brooklyn Elevated Railroad Company, the party of the second part hereto hath likewise caused these present to be subscribed by its President and its corporate seal to be hereto affixed, and Frederick Uhlmann, the Receiver of the said party of the second part, hath on the same day and likewise in witness thereof and by direction of the Supreme Court of the State of New York, granting permission and authority to him so to do, for and on behalf of the said Railroad Company of which he is such Receiver, likewise subscribed these presents and caused his seal to be thereto attached.

THE TRUSTEES OF THE NEW YORK AND BROOKLYN BRIDGE,

By WILLIAM BERRI,
President.

In presence of:
Attest:
HENRY BEAM,
Secretary.

BROOKLYN ELEVATED RAILROAD COMPANY,
By FREDERICK UHLMANN,

Attest: President.
ELISHA DYER, JR.,
Secretary.
FREDERICK UHLMANN,
Receiver.

STATE OF NEW YORK, ⎫
  City of Brooklyn, ⎬ *ss.:*
  County of Kings, ⎭

On this twenty-third day of August, eighteen hundred and ninety-seven, before me personally came William Berri, to me known, who being by me duly sworn, did depose and say that he resided in the City of Brooklyn; that he was the President of the Trustees of the New York and Brooklyn Bridge, the corporation described in and which executed the foregoing instrument; that he knew the corporate seal of said Trustees of the New York and Brooklyn Bridge; that the seal affixed to the foregoing instrument was such corporate seal; that it was affixed by order of said Trustees, and that he signed his name thereto as President by like authority.

               A. F. BRITTON,
                    Notary Public,
                        Kings County.

STATE OF NEW YORK, ⎫
  City of Brooklyn, ⎬ *ss.:*
  County of Kings, ⎭

On this twenty-third day of August, in the year eighteen hundred and ninety-seven, before me personally came Frederick Uhlmann, to me personally known, who being by me duly sworn, did depose and say that he resided in the City of New York; that he was the President of the Brooklyn Elevated Railroad Company, the corporation described in and which executed the foregoing instrument; that he knew the corporate seal of the said Railroad Company; that the seal affixed to the foregoing instrument was such corporate seal; that it was affixed by order of the Board of Directors of the said Brooklyn Elevated Railroad Company, and that he signed his name thereto by the like order as President of the said Brooklyn Elevated Railroad Company.

               A. F. BRITTON,
                    Notary Public,
                        Kings County.

STATE OF NEW YORK, ⎫
  City of Brooklyn, ⎬ *ss.:*
  County of Kings, ⎭

    On this twenty-third day of August, eighteen hundred and ninety-seven, before me personally came Frederick Uhlmann, to me personally known, who being by me duly sworn, did depose and say that he resided in the City of New York; that he was the Receiver of the Brooklyn Elevated Railroad Company; that he executed the foregoing instrument for and on behalf of the said Brooklyn Elevated Railroad Company, in his capacity as Receiver thereof, by subscribing his name and affixing his seal thereto, and that such execution by him was made and done pursuant to the provisions of an order of the Supreme Court of the State of New York, made on the 17th day of August, 1897, in the matter entitled, whereby deponent as such Receiver was authorized to make and enter into, execute and acknowledge the said foregoing instrument.

                A. F. BRITTON,
                        Notary Public,
                              Kings County.

AGREEMENT (ORIGINAL).

THE KINGS COUNTY ELEVATED RAILWAY CO.

THIS AGREEMENT, made this 23d day of August, 1897, between THE TRUSTEES OF THE NEW YORK AND BROOKLYN BRIDGE, party of the first part, and THE KINGS COUNTY ELEVATED RAILWAY COMPANY, party of the second part, WITNESSETH:

That the party of the first part, for and in consideration of the payments to be made to it by the party of the second part, and of the faithful, just and full performance of the undertakings, covenants and agreements to be by said party of the second part performed and carried out as hereinafter set forth, doth, subject to the conditions and restrictions herein provided and expressed, grant and lease to the party of the second part the right and privilege to enter upon the premises of the party of the first part with its cars for the transportation of passengers, and to have the cars of said party of the second part, and the passengers using and traveling in said cars transported and operated by the party of the first part across its Bridge; and to that end to cross, intersect, join and unite its railroad with the railroad operated by the party of the first part upon and across the New York and Brooklyn Bridge, subject, however, in all things in such crossing, intersecting, joining and uniting to the control and direction of the Chief Engineer of the party of the first part; the terms upon which this lease, license, privilege or grant is made, the conditions subject to which the rights hereby conferred upon the party of the second part are to be exercised, and the covenants by said party of the second part to be observed and performed, are as follows, to wit:

I.—The said Railway Company shall arrange for the connection of its tracks with the tracks of the New York and Brooklyn Bridge at some point at or north of Tillary street, in the City of Brooklyn, to be determined upon by the Chief Engineer of the party of the first part and convenient for that purpose, so that the trains of said company shall approach and enter the property of the said Trustees upon a single track, which shall be connected with the north tracks now owned and controlled by the said Trustees over said Bridge, and so that the trains of said Company on returning from New York shall leave the property of the said Trustees upon a single track, which shall be connected with the south tracks, now owned and controlled by the Trustees, over said Bridge in such manner as may be designated by the Chief Engineer of said Bridge.

The said Trustees shall permit the said Railway Company to bring its empty cars and trains to the present or any subsequently constructed outgoing platform of the Trustees in the New York station which may be by the said Trustees designated, or the construction of which may be permitted, and there to reecive passengers for transportation to Brooklyn. All platforms used or to be used by the party of the second part shall be so used subject to the control and use thereof by the said Trustees, and any platforms subsequently constructed pursuant to permission of said Trustees for the use of said party of the second part, together with the stairways thereof, shall be constructed at such points as shall be designated by the Chief Engineer of the party of the first part.

Said Railroad Company shall prepare the plans for such connections, and do and pay for the work, provided only that said plans shall be approved by the Chief Engineer of the party of the first part and the work be carried on subject to his approval and inspection, and such plans are those hereto attached, which it is hereby covenanted are and constitute a part of this agreement.

II.—The location of the said tracks and of the curves and switches necessary to connect the present tracks of the said railway with the tracks of the said Bridge, and all constructions of every kind necessary to the use of the said tracks, as herein provided, shall be under the absolute control and direction of the Chief Engineer of the said Bridge, and no construction of any kind connected therewith or relating thereto shall be had or used unless the plan or plans therefor have been first submitted to the said Engineer, and have been approved by him and are hereto attached, as aforesaid.

III.—The expenses of all changes necessary in the construction upon the said Bridge or the approach thereto, in order to permit the delivery of the cars of the said Elevated Railway Company to the control of the said Trustees of the Bridge, and to permit the transportation thereof and return thereof to said Railway Company, and the maintenance and repairing of all changes and additions aforesaid, shall be borne and paid by the said Railway Company. Provided, that the cost of whatever part of such construction which shall be used by more than one railroad company, or the necessity for the creation of which shall be common to the bringing upon the Bridge of cars of more than one railroad company, shall be borne by the several railroad companies in such shares and proportions as they may agree upon, or, if they fail to agree, in such shares and proportions as the Trustees of the said Bridge may determine.

All plans and contracts for labor and material necessary to the construction aforesaid of the approaches to the premises of the Trustees, and to the entry upon and departure from said premises by said Railway Company, shall be made by said Railway Company in its own name and upon its own responsibility; all material necessary to be used upon the premises of the Trustees shall be supplied by said Railway Company, and all labor to be performed upon said premises shall be performed by said Railroad Company, and the cost thereof paid by said Railway Company, before entering said premises with its cars. All of such work and material shall be subject to approval and rejection by the said Trustees; all of such construction upon property belonging to the Trustees of the New York and Brooklyn Bridge shall become and be the property of the said The Trustees of the New York and Brooklyn Bridge, when and as soon as work shall be begun or material necessary to such construction shall be delivered upon premises of said party of the first part, all work done in pursuance of the terms of this contract by said Railway Company, shall be so carried on as in no manner to interfere with, limit or obstruct the operation of the railroad of and belonging to said Trustees upon and over said Bridge.

IV.—All rights of way, franchises and property necessary to be secured in order to construct the tracks upon which to enter upon and leave the said Bridge property shall be secured and paid for by the said Railway Company.

V.—Each car, except motor cars, of the said Elevated Railway Company intended to be used upon the railroad of the Bridge shall be equipped with grips in form and construction as may be designated by the Chief Engineer of the Bridge, together with the same appliances for braking while on the Bridge as employed upon the cars of the Trustees of the Bridge, or as directed by said Chief Engineer. One car on each train shall also be equipped with electric motors on each truck identical with those adopted by the Bridge Trustees, or as may be suggested and approved by the Chief Engineer of the Bridge, for the purpose of switching trains at termini. All elevated railway cars sent or used upon the Bridge shall have side doors, in form and construction to be approved by said Chief Engineer.

VI.—All cars used on the Bridge service, and all equipment and appliances relating thereto, located on Bridge property, shall be subject at all times to inspection by the Bridge authorities, who shall have power to forbid rights on the Bridge to cars that may, for any reason, be unsatisfactory, and to direct the removal of any old or inadequate equipment or appliances, and the substitution therefor of others of approved character. On arriving at the place nearest to the point where the cars of said Railway Company shall enter upon the premises of the Trustees of the Bridge, as the same shall be fixed and located by the said Bridge Trustees the locomotives shall be detached from the trains upon the said elevated railway, and such trains shall then be propelled by the electric motor cars, already referred to, over such tracks as the Trustees of the said Bridge shall designate to the point at which the cable is lifted into grips, from which point the train shall proceed over the Bridge by cable traction precisely as the cars of the Bridge Railway are now operated; and on returning from New York the said trains after passing the unloading platforms at the Brooklyn terminal of the said Bridge shall be propelled by the electric motor car as aforesaid, to the place upon the track of the said Elevated Railway Company selected by the Chief Engineer of the party of the first part. From the time when the trains of the said Railway Company enter upon the premises of said Trustees until on the return of the trains from New York, they shall depart from said premises, said cars and trains shall be under the exclusive management and control of the Trustees of the New York and Brooklyn Bridge and of their employees.

VII.—The said Trustees shall have full and complete power to make and adopt all other rules and regulations which to them shall seem reasonable and proper relating to the transporting of the cars of the said Railway Company over the said Bridge, including the method of payment of tolls, the style of cars to be used, and the condition of the cars, the switching of cars, and the use of platform, and to amend or alter any of such rules or regulations so as to secure the safety and comfort of persons using the said Bridge, and to subserve the purpose for which said Bridge was constructed; but the Railroad Company shall be allowed to place and retain advertising signs inside its cars.

The Railroad Company shall not bring upon the premises of the party of the first part or deliver to them for transportation across the Bridge, any cars in which smoking shall be permitted while the cars of the said Railroad Company are upon the premises of the party of the first part.

VIII.—The said Railway Company shall pay to the said Trustees of the New York and Brooklyn Bridge the sum of twelve and one-half cents per round trip for each car transported as aforesaid, provided that if at any time the regulations adopted by the said Trustees shall be altered or modified so as to permit the said Railway Company to operate cars across said Bridge by their own power, the said Railway Company shall pay the sum of five cents per round trip for each car so operated; provided that, pursuant to the provisions of chapter 663, Laws of 1897, the said party of the second part shall not by reason of the payments by it to be made to the party of the first part as herein provided or otherwise, or for any reason whatsoever, " charge any fare in excess of, or additional to, the fare exacted by it from any passenger for one continuous ride upon any of the routes in either of the cities of New York or Brooklyn, as the case may be, so that the said route of said corporation operated across said Bridge hereunder, so far as the exaction of a fare is concerned, shall be taken and deemed to be a part of the continuous route, or one of the continuous routes, of the said Railroad corporation whereon one fare is exacted, so that no extra or additional fare shall be exacted by said party of the second part from any passenger carried to or from the Bridge and across the Bridge in addition to the fare exacted from such passenger for carriage to and from the Bridge only."

IX.—All trains coming upon the premises of the party of the first part shall, when approaching an intersection with any track of said party of the first part, be brought to a full stop before crossing the same, and shall not be again started until signal to proceed be given by a man employed for such purpose by said party of the first part.

X.—The said Railroad Company shall protect and hold harmless the said Trustees from and against all losses, damages and claims for damages, actions, recoveries, costs, disbursements and expenses of every nature arising from, based upon, connected with, or in any manner charged to be due to injury to person or property received or sustained by any person upon and in the cars of the said Company whenever and wherever upon the premises of said Trustees such injuries may arise, be received or sustained, or which may be caused by the cars of the said Railroad Company, or which may arise from or be connected with the presence and operation of such cars upon such premises or which shall in any wise be connected with or arise out of the bringing of the said cars upon the premises of the party of the first part, or transporting or operating them, upon, over or across the same, or which may arise from or be connected with the making, building, construction, erecting, or changing of any work, of every kind necessary for the bringing of the cars of the party of the second part upon the said Bridge and the operating and the transporting of the same across the said Bridge, or in any and every wise growing out of the use of the said Bridge and of the premises, appurtenances and appliances thereunto belonging by the party of the second part.

And the said Railroad Company shall further protect and hold harmless the said Trustees from and against losses, damages and claims for damages, actions, recoveries, costs, disbursements and expense of every nature which may arise or result from any failure or delay on the part of the said Railroad Company to promptly and regularly operate and transport its cars across said Bridge in either direction, or for any delay or hindrance to said cars while in transit, from whatever cause or reason such neglect or refusal or delay may arise, or which may arise to any person using the said Bridge in any way or manner, who shall be injured in person or property, or hindered or delayed in the use of said Bridge by reason of any matter, thing or occurrence arising from or connected with the operation of the cars across the said structure. And, should there at any time occur a block upon the roadway of said Bridge, or interference with the use of said roadway by the public by reason of the operation of the cars of the said Railroad Company across the Bridge, the said Railroad Company shall protect and hold harmless the said Trustees from and against all claims or damages resulting from the same. And should there be caused by the operation of the said cars, or in any connected therewith, any accident upon such roadway, the said Railroad Company shall in like manner protect and hold harmless the said Trustees against losses, damages, and claims for damages, actions, recoveries, costs, disbursements and expenses of every nature, which may arise therefrom.

And the said Railroad Company shall further protect and hold harmless said Trustees from and against any and all suits, lets, hindrances, actions, recoveries, claims, damages, costs, disbursements and expenses of every kind, nature, amount and description, which may arise, be made and presented, brought, instituted, sustained or recovered on the ground of deprivation of owners of property adjoining premises of the party of the first part of light, or air, or interruption of either, or of damages of any and every nature consequent upon and resulting from the bringing of the cars of said Railroad upon premises of party of the first part and operating the same thereupon, and over said premises and Bridge.

But nothing herein is to be construed as rendering the party of the second part liable to the Trustees or to any person, firm or corporation, for any damages, injury or hindrance, or render it liable to suffer any recovery against it by said Trustees for any delay or accident arising solely from faulty construction or imperfect track or appurtenance of or connected with the Bridge or solely from negligence on the part of the agents or servants of the Trustees.

XI.—The supervision, management and control of cars of the Railway Company shall in every particular and at all times be wholly exercised by the Trustees of the New York and Brooklyn Bridge within the discretion and at the dictation of the Chief Engineer of said Trustees from the delivery of said cars upon the premises of the Trustees till their departure therefrom, provided, only, that while said Chief Engineer shall at all times regulate and limit in his discretion the number of cars of the Railway Company which may be operated as aforesaid, nevertheless inasmuch as it is in contemplation by the parties hereto that privileges similar to those herein set forth are to be granted to the Brooklyn Elevated Railroad Company, the number of cars of the Kings County Railway Company to be operated upon and over said Bridge shall not be limited to less than one car of the Kings County Elevated Railway Company to two cars of the Brooklyn Elevated Railroad Company.

It is hereby mutually covenanted and agreed that no delay, hindrance or refusal to receive and operate cars of the Kings County Railway Company shall be made or exercised by reason of failure for any reason on the part of the Brooklyn Elevated Railroad Company to deliver its quota of cars upon the premises of the Trustees regularly and promptly in accordance with any schedule or rule of operation which may be promulgated by said Chief Engineer.

AND WHEREAS, the exercise of the right to cause its cars to be operated across the Bridge necessitates the surrender by the Trustees to such use of one set of tracks for such purpose, thereby reducing the number of Bridge trains which it is possible for said Trustees to operate, now therefore, it is hereby mutually agreed that the number of trains and cars to be delivered by said Railway Company to said Trustees shall at all times equal one-half the number of trains and cars belonging to said Trustees and operated by them, at the date of the execution of these presents, provided only, that should the Brooklyn Elevated Railroad secure from said Trustees provisions similar to those hereby granted, the said party of the second part may reduce the number of cars to be delivered by it to not less than one-sixth the number operated by said Trustees at the date of the execution of these presents.

XII.—The term of the right and privilege hereby granted to the party of the second part to enter upon the premises of the party of the first part with its cars for the transportation of passengers, and to have its cars and the passengers using and traveling in the same transported and operated by the said Trustees across its Bridge, and to that end to cross, intersect, join and unite its railroad with the railroad operated by the party of the first part, shall be terminable at the option of either party hereto after expiration of ten years from the date when this contract shall be duly executed, provided only that, if, in the opinion of the party of the first part, or its legal successors, and of the Mayor of The City of New York, and of the President of the Borough of Brooklyn, to be hereafter elected pursuant to the provisions of chapter 378 of the Laws of 1897, or in the opinion of the majority of them, it should be determined that it is against the public interest to continue the operation of the trains or cars of the party of the second part, upon, over and across the Bridge, or if the said party of the second part should for itself determine that the facilities afforded it are inadequate for its passenger service, then, and in that event, this agreement and all of the rights and privileges granted to said party of the second part and obligations assumed by it, shall be terminable on and after three months' notice in writing by either party to the other that it elects to determine said contract.

XIII.—The said Railway Company before entering in any manner upon the premises of the party of the first part for the performance of any work necessary to make the connection hereinbefore provided for shall execute and deliver to the Trustees of said Bridge its bond in the sum of fifty thousand dollars and in such form with such sureties as the Trustees shall prescribe (which bond shall be approved as to form and manner of execution and sufficiency of sureties by the Counsel of said Trustees) conditioned that the said Company shall promptly complete the work entered upon by it as hereinbefore provided, and if it shall fail so to do that it shall pay to said Trustees of said Bridge the necessary expenses of completing the same or of removing any portions of said structures which are upon the property of the said the Trustees of the

Bridge, and of restoring the Bridge and all the premises of the party of the first part, and all things appurtenant thereto, to the present condition, whichever the said Trustees shall elect to do; and further conditioned that the said Railway Company shall observe, obey and keep each and every rule and regulation made and adopted by the said Trustees as hereinbefore provided, and for the discharge of any and all liability hereby imposed and which may arise or be incurred pursuant to the provisions of this contract; and further conditioned that the said Railway Company shall and will faithfully, promptly and fully pay to said Trustees the rental hereby reserved and the charges hereby imposed.

And for a failure and neglect to observe, obey and keep such rules and regulations, or any of them, and for failure to promptly make payment to said Trustees of the said rental reserved and charges by this agreement imposed, the said Trustees may revoke the said agreement so far as it affects the said Railway Company, and thereupon said Railway Company shall forfeit all rights and privileges heretofore enjoyed thereunder.

XIV.—It is hereby covenanted, agreed and understood that the foregoing agreement in all its parts does and is intended to apply to the Kings County Railway Company, and to any and all companies which as the result of the reorganization of said company now pending may be and become the legal successor to said company and owner of its rights, privileges and franchises, and to James Jourdan, Esq., as Receiver of the corporate rights, franchises and properties of said Kings County Railway Company and to any and all successors in office of said James Jourdan as Receiver, and that in order to be effectual and binding this instrument shall be executed by the officers of said Railway Company and by said Receiver.

It is further covenanted that said Receiver shall before executing this agreement, obtain the consent of the Supreme Court having control and jurisdiction of and over the acts of such Receiver to the execution thereof.

XV.—The said Railway Company doth hereby further covenant, promise and agree, that for and in consideration of the provisions of this instrument and of the privileges and grants thereby extended to it by the party of the first part, it will commence the work preparatory to the exercise of the privileges hereby extended within sixty days after the date of the execution of this instrument, and that all of said work hereinbefore provided for as necessary to the operation of the cars of the said Railway Company over the Bridge shall be fully completed, and said operation of cars be regularly commenced within one year after the date of the execution of these presents, provided only, that should either the commencement, continuation or finishing of such work or the operation of the cars of the said Railway Company upon, over and across the premises of the party of the first part be delayed by litigation, strikes or causes of delay not created by the party of the second part, and not to be avoided by ordinary precautions on its part, the time necessarily consumed in such litigation and by such strikes or causes of delay aforesaid, shall be added to the time herein provided for the beginning and completion of the work aforesaid; and further provided, that for failure to comply with the provision of this agreement, or by reason of the institution by or at the instigation of the said Railway Company of litigation of any nature, instituted in any wise for the purpose of increasing the time within which the provisions of this contract shall be put in effect, the said party of the first part, may, at the discretion of said Trustees revoke each and every privilege hereinbefore contained and set forth, and upon such revocation all work and material put upon the premises of the party of the first part by said Railway Company shall be and become forfeit to the said Trustees without damage or compensation therefor to the said Railway Company.

It is hereby covenanted and agreed, that the said Railway Company shall not in any way enter upon the premises of the party of the first part or commence any work or construction thereon, nor place any material to be used in such work and construction upon the premises of the party of the first part, until all the work and construction to be undertaken and performed by the party of the second part outside of the property of the said Trustees, and necessary and sufficient for the purpose of making the connection between the railway of the said party of the second part and that of the said Trustees, as hereinbefore provided, shall be fairly under way to the end that all construction necessary to cross the Bridge by cars of the aforesaid railroad may be completed at about the same time; nor shall said Railroad Company enter upon or do any work of construction upon the premises of said Trustees until it shall have secured its right-of-way and removed any and every injunction that may have been granted by a Court of competent jurisdiction, and also that the said Railway Company shall not in any way interfere with the operation of the railroad operated by the Trustees, pending construction necessary to connect the railroad of the party of the second part with the Bridge and permit its cars to be operated thereon, nor shall said Railway Company use the structure of the Bridge for the storage of material to be used in such work and construction, nor permit its employees or the employees of contractors to use the Bridge premises as a rendezvous or resting place, but work of construction is to proceed day by day without interruption, except if the Railroad Company is enjoined from proceeding by the Court, or in the event of strikes or hindrances or delays beyond the control of the Railroad Company, and it is expressly stipulated that in all matters connected with construction and work on the premises of the Trustees, that the Chief Engineer of the Bridge shall have absolute supervision and control.

IN WITNESS WHEREOF, on the 23d day of August, Eighteen hundred and ninety-seven, the party of the first part, the Trustees of the New York and Brooklyn Bridge, has caused these presents to be subscribed by its President and its corporate seal to be hereto affixed, and on the same day the said Kings County Elevated Railway Company, the party of the second part hereto, hath likewise caused these presents to be subscribed by its President and its corporate seal to be hereto affixed, and James Jourdan, the Receiver of the said party of the second part, hath on the same day and likewise in witness thereof and by direction of the Supreme Court of the State of New York, granting permission and authority to him so to do, for and on behalf of the said Railroad Company of which he is such Receiver, likewise subscribe these presents and caused his seal to be hereto attached.

THE TRUSTEES OF THE NEW YORK AND BROOKLYN BRIDGE,

By WILLIAM BERRI, President.

In presence of—

Attest:

HENRY BEAM,
    Secretary. [SEAL.]

H. J. ROBINSON,
    Secretary.

THE KINGS COUNTY ELEVATED RAILWAY COMPANY,

By JAMES JOURDAN,
    President.
JAMES JOURDAN,
    Receiver.

STATE OF NEW YORK,
  City of Brooklyn, } *ss.:*
  County of Kings,

On this twenty-third day of August, in the year eighteen hundred and ninety-seven, before me personally came William Berri, to me personally known, who being by me duly sworn, did depose and say that he resided in the City of Brooklyn; that he was the President of The Trustees of the New York and Brooklyn Bridge, the corporation described in and which executed the foregoing instrument; that he knew the corporate seal of the said The Trustees of the New York and Brooklyn Bridge; that the seal affixed to the foregoing instrument was such corporate seal; that it was affixed by order of said Trustees, and that he signed his name thereto as President by the like order.

A. F. BRITTON,
    Notary Public,
        Kings County.

STATE OF NEW YORK, ⎫
  City of Brooklyn, ⎬ *ss.:*
  County of Kings, ⎭

On this twenty-third day of August, in the year eighteen hundred and ninety-seven, before me personally came James Jourdan, to me personally known, who being by me duly sworn, did depose and say that he resided in Edgewater, Richmond County, N. Y.; that he was the President of the Kings County Elevated Railway Company, the corporation described in and which executed the foregoing instrument; that he knew the corporate seal of the said Railway Company; that the seal affixed to the foregoing instrument was such corporate seal; that it was affixed by order of the Board of Directors of the said Kings County Elevated Railway Company, and that he signed his name thereto by the like order as President of the said Kings County Elevated Railway Company.

                A. F. BRITTON,
                      Notary Public,
                          Kings County.

STATE OF NEW YORK, ⎫
  City of Brooklyn, ⎬ *ss.:*
  County of Kings, ⎭

On this twenty-third day of August, eighteen hundred and ninety-seven, before me personally came James Jourdan, to me personally known, who being by me duly sworn, did depose and say that he resided in Edgewater, Richmond County, N. Y.; that he was the Receiver of the Kings County Elevated Railway Company; that he executed the foregoing agreement for and on behalf of the said Kings County Elevated Railway Company, in his capacity as Receiver thereof, by subscribing his name and affixing his seal thereto, and that such execution by him was made and done pursuant to the provisions of an order of the Supreme Court of the State of New York, made on the 19th day of August, 1897, in the matter entitled, whereby deponent as such Receiver was authorized to make and enter into, execute and acknowledge the said foregoing instrument.

                A. F. BRITTON,
                      Notary Public,
                          Kings County.

AGREEMENTS (MODIFIED)

BROOKLYN ELEVATED RAILROAD COMPANY

AND

THE KINGS COUNTY ELEVATED RAILWAY CO.

THIS AGREEMENT, made this twenty-third day of June, 1898, by and between JOHN L. SHEA, Commissioner of Bridges of The City of New York (hereinafter called the "Commissioner"), of the first part, and FREDERICK UHLMANN, Receiver of the Brooklyn Elevated Railroad Company (hereinafter called the "RECEIVER") and the said BROOKLYN ELEVATED RAILROAD COMPANY, parties of the second part. (It being understood that the term the "Brooklyn" when hereafter used shall include the "Receiver," any person who may be appointed in his place and any successor company that may be organized to operate the "Brooklyn" Elevated Railroad Company, the Union Elevated Railroad Company (hereinafter called "The Union") and the Sea Side and Brooklyn Bridge Elevated Railroad Company (hereinafter called the "Seaside"), after the sale under the foreclosure of the several mortgages of the respective properties and franchises of such several railroads):

WHEREAS, an agreement was heretofore duly executed between the Trustees of the New York and Brooklyn Bridge and the "Brooklyn," dated the 23d day of August, 1897, in which contract the said "Receiver" joined in pursuance of the authority of the Supreme Court, providing for the operation of the cars of the "Brooklyn" over one set of the gauntleted tracks of the railroad upon the New York and Brooklyn Bridge, the other set of such tracks being reserved for the operation by said Trustees of the railroad running between the termini of said Bridge (hereinafter called the "Local Railroad"), a copy of which contract is hereto annexed; and,

WHEREAS, by a contract bearing the same date, executed between said Trustees of the New York and Brooklyn Bridge and the Kings County Elevated Railway Company (hereinafter called the " Kings ") and its Receiver, the said " Kings " was also authorized to operate its cars over the same set of said tracks as those authorized to be used by the " Brooklyn," and to construct and operate a connection between the same and the structure of the " Kings " in Fulton street, in the Borough of Brooklyn, City of New York; and,

WHEREAS, by said two contracts the operation of the cars of the " Brooklyn " and of the " Kings " over said set of tracks and their connections on said Bridge was to be carried on under the supervision and direction of the Bridge authorities, and by both cable traction and electricity, and the trains of said railroads while upon said Bridge were required to be under the exclusive management and control of said Trustees and of their employees, and while the " Brooklyn " was to hold said Trustees harmless from all damage from the presence upon the Bridge of its cars or their transportation over the same, yet that said Trustees should remain liable for accidents arising from the faulty construction or imperfections in either the tracks or appurtenances connected with the Bridge, and for negligence of the agents or servants of said Trustees controlling the said trains; and,

WHEREAS, in and by said contract it was further agreed that the number of trains and cars to be delivered by the " Brooklyn " and the " Kings " to the Trustees shall be equal to one-half the number of trains and cars belonging to said Trustees and operated by them upon said " Local Railroad " at the date of said contract, of which number at least two-thirds should be so delivered by the " Brooklyn " and one-third by the " Kings "; and,

WHEREAS, the platform upon said Bridge to be used by the " Brooklyn " under said contract has been constructed and the connections between the Bridge and the structure of the said " Brooklyn " are so far completed that the cars of the " Brooklyn " will be operated over said Bridge within a short time; and,

WHEREAS, said contract provides that the " Brooklyn " shall pay for the operation of its cars over said Bridge, for the service of the Bridge employees having control of such cars while they are upon said Bridge, and for the use of the cable and electric power belonging to said Bridge the sum of twelve and one-half cents per round trip for each car hauled over said Bridge; and,

WHEREAS, it is provided in said contract that in case the regulations of said Trustees shall be altered or modified so as to permit the "Brooklyn" to operate cars across said Bridge by its own power, it shall pay the sum of five cents per round trip for each car so operated; and,

WHEREAS, at the time of the execution of said contracts with the "Brooklyn" and the "Kings" contracts were also made between the said Trustees of the New York and Brooklyn Bridge and the Brooklyn Heights Railroad Company, the Nassau Electric Railroad Company and various other street surface railroads in the City of Brooklyn, authorizing them to operate their respective cars over the driveways of said Bridge, in pursuance whereof tracks have been so laid in said driveways and said street surface railroads are operating their cars over the same by the trolley system; and,

WHEREAS, since the operation of the cars of the surface railroads over the said driveways the number of passengers using the "Local Railroad" operated by the "Commissioner" has decreased until the same is now less than one-half of the number of such passengers who were transported over said "Local Railroad" prior to the operation of said surface cars on the driveway of said Bridge, which reduction has so diminished the receipts of said "Local Railroad" as to render its operation unprofitable, and when the cars of the "Brooklyn" and of the "Kings" shall be operated over such Bridge, the earnings of said "Local Railroad" will be further greatly diminished, so that the accountants of the said "Commissioner" have estimated and reported to him that notwithstanding the tolls provided to be paid by the respective surface and elevated railroads under the contracts made by them with the said Trustees, and all and every other income which may be received by the "Commissioner" from the said Bridge, the operation of the said "Local Railroad" by him, if continued and the aforesaid agreements of August 23, 1897, with said several surface and elevated railroads remain in force will involve an annual loss to The City of New York of upwards of $600,000; and,

WHEREAS, the said "Commissioner," who has succeeded to the powers and duties of the Trustees of the New York and Brooklyn Bridge, has expressed dissatisfaction with said contract between said Trustees and the "Brooklyn," and has required that the same shall be altered to the end that The City of New York shall realize a larger amount than that prescribed in said contract for the operation of the cars of the "Brooklyn" over said Bridge, and has also required the assumption by the "Brooklyn" of the operation of the "Local Railroad" of the Bridge, so as to relieve the said "Commissioner" from the expense of operating the same and of furnishing power and employees to said "Brooklyn"; and,

WHEREAS, the "Brooklyn" has agreed to assume these obligations upon the terms and conditions herein provided; and also to pay an increased price for the operation of its cars over the set of tracks reserved for elevated railroads; and,

WHEREAS, the said "Brooklyn" is in the possession of and is being operated by said Frederick Uhlmann, who has been appointed Receiver thereof in certain foreclosure suits instituted by the Central Trust Company of New York, as Trustee, against the said Brooklyn Elevated Railroad Company and the Union Elevated Railroad Company, respectively, and in said actions and in a similar action brought by the said Central Trust Company against the Seaside and Brooklyn Bridge Elevated Railroad Company, the rights and franchises of the said "Brooklyn," the "Union" and the "Seaside" will be sold and will, it is expected, be acquired by a new corporation to be formed by the purchasers; and;

WHEREAS, Frederic P. Olcott, James T. Woodward, Charles Parsons, Ernst Thalman and Leonard Lewisohn, the Reorganization Committee, who are the holders of nearly all the bonds of the "Brooklyn" and of the "Union" and the "Seaside," as also of the great majority of the shares of the capital stock of the "Brooklyn," and who, as the holders of such securities, intend to become the purchasers at said foreclosure sale and to organize said new Corporation, have approved of this agreement, and requested the execution thereof by said "Receiver"; and,

WHEREAS, the safety, comfort and convenience of the traveling public are intended to be and will be greatly enhanced, and it is estimated that instead of The City of New York being compelled to meet a large deficiency from the operation of the said Bridge, it will secure a considerable surplus of revenue therefrom, if the agreements of August 23, 1897, are modified, and if the operation of the "Local Railroad" shall be assumed by the "Brooklyn" as herein provided;

Now, THEREFORE, THIS AGREEMENT, WITNESSETH, that in consideration of the premises, of the mutual agreements hereinafter contained and of the sum of one dollar paid by each of the parties hereto to the other, the receipt whereof is hereby acknowledged, it is HEREBY MUTUALLY AGREED by and between the parties hereto as follows:

PART I.—THE "BROOKLYN" to UNDERTAKE THE OPERATION OF THE "LOCAL RAILROAD" ON THE BRIDGE.

First—The "Brooklyn" hereby agrees that it will during the existence of this agreement, at its own expense, operate the "Local Railroad" between the termini of said Bridge, which is now operated by said "Commissioner," upon the set of gauntleted tracks upon said Bridge reserved for the use of said "Local Railroad," in pursuance of the agreements heretofore made between the Trustees of the said Bridge and the "Receiver" and the "Brooklyn" and between said Trustees and the "Kings" and James Jourdan, its Receiver, and will furnish, fix the wages of and pay all necessary employees, and in all things assume and carry out the obligations of said Commissioner," with regard to properly operating the same, for the term and in the manner hereinafter specially set forth, and shall at all times faithfully keep and observe on its part all and singular the stipulations and agreements hereinafter set forth relating to adequate train service in the interests of the public, as well as the payment of the tolls and revenues provided for herein. Inasmuch as by the through service which will be rendered by the operation of the cars of the "Brooklyn" and of the "Kings" both over said Bridge and over the said elevated railroads, respectively, for a single fare of five cents, the number of passengers using the said "Local Railroad" will be largely diminished, it is agreed that the number of trains to be operated over said " Local Railroad " by the " Brooklyn " may from time to time be increased or diminished by it to conform to the requirements of the traveling public passing between these termini. It shall not be incumbent upon the " Brooklyn " to operate special trains upon said " Local Railroad " between said termini of the Bridge during those hours of the day and night when travel shall be light. Provided, however, that whenever such special trains during said hours shall be discontinued, the " Brooklyn " must operate through cars and trains which will also furnish adequate facilities for such of the public as desire only to travel between the termini of the " Local Railroad " of the Bridge. Special trains shall, however, be operated upon the said " Local Railroad " during the " rush hours " of the morning and evening of week days. The " Commissioner," however, shall be the judge of what is such adequate train service, and in the interests of the traveling public may require that the present facilities shall not be curtailed or diminished.

Second—The " Commissioner " shall personally or by his appointees, inspect and supervise the operation of the said " Local Railroad " by the said " Brooklyn " and give such directions in relation thereto as will insure proper service to the public. All of the employees of the " Brooklyn " in the operation of said " Local Railroad " shall be subject to the approval of the " Commissioner " and no appointee shall be retained by the " Brooklyn " in connection with the operation of the said " Local Railroad " if the said " Commissioner " shall find that he is an unfit person for such purpose.

Third —The said " Commissioner " shall designate the switchmen to operate the tower and other switches on the tracks of said " Local Railroad," and also the switchmen to operate the switches at the places where the railroads of the " Brooklyn " and " Kings " shall cross the tracks of said Bridge in entering and leaving the same in the Bridge yard. The appointments of such switchmen shall, however, be approved by the " Brooklyn " and no one shall be appointed or retained in such capacity if he shall be objected to by the " Brooklyn " as not being competent for that purpose. The wages of such switchmen shall be fixed and paid by the " Brooklyn."

Fourth—Whenever both the Elevated and "Local Railroad" trains shall be operated over said Bridge in the "rush hours" of the morning and evening, during week days, the "Brooklyn" is required, in order to avoid all danger of collision, to use in operating such cars over the said Bridge, the cable and grips, together with electric power such as is now used in such operation. At all other hours of the day and night, the use of the cable and grips, may at the option of the "Brooklyn" be discontinued, provided that such discontinuance shall not in the judgment of the "Commissioner" be detrimental to the traveling public.

Fifth—The rate of fare to be charged to passengers who may be transported by the "Brooklyn" between said termini only, whether the same be in special trains of the "Local Railroad" or in the through trains of the "Brooklyn" shall be three cents for a single passage or five cents for two tickets, as is now charged by the "Commissioner" and such tickets shall be transferrable.

Sixth—The "Brooklyn" agrees that it will during the continuance of this agreement, keep special books of account which shall at all times be open to the inspection of the "Commissioner" or any accountant to be appointed by him and which shall set forth all receipts arising from the operation of the "Local Railroad." From said receipts there shall be deducted the moneys paid by the "Brooklyn" for such operation, including salaries, wages to employees, material, cost of maintenance and the general expenses connected therewith. The difference will be entered in such books as surplus or deficit, as the case may be. If, at the end of any fiscal year, there shall be a deficit, the "Brooklyn" is to bear the same and make no charge whatever for reimbursement of any part thereof against the "Commissioner." If, on the other hand, there shall be a surplus, the "Commissioner" shall be entitled to receive from said surplus, as follows:

Five per cent. (5%) thereof, if over ten thousand dollars ($10,000) and under twenty thousand dollars ($20,000).

Seven and one-half per cent. (7½%) if over twenty thousand dollars ($20,000) and up to forty thousand dollars ($40,000).

Ten per cent. (10%) if over forty thousand dollars ($40,000) and up to sixty thousand dollars ($60,000).

Twelve and one-half per cent. (12½%) if over sixty thousand dollars ($60,000) and up to eighty thousand dollars, ($80,000).

Fifteen per cent. (15%) if over eighty thousand dollars ($80,000) and up to one hundred thousand dollars ($100,000).

Twenty per cent. (20%) if over one hundred thousand dollars ($100,000) and up to one hundred and fifty thousand dollars ($150,000).

Twenty-five per cent (25%) on all amounts exceeding one hundred and fifty thousand dollars ($150,000).

To the end that the "Commissioner" is to receive, in any event, without any deduction whatever, on account of the losses which may be sustained by the operation of the "Local Railroad" in any year, all and any income coming to him under this agreement or any other source of income connected with said Bridge, and that in case any profits shall be derived from the operation of said "Local Railroad" he shall be entitled to participate therein as hereinabove mentioned.

Seventh—The said "Commissioner" acting for and on behalf of The City of New York, and for and in consideration of the payments to be made to him by the "Brooklyn" and of the faithful, just and full performance of the several undertakings, covenants and agreements to be by it carried out as herein set forth, has authorized and does hereby authorize the said "Brooklyn" subject to the reservations herein provided, to operate the said "Local Railroad" over said tracks and between the termini of the said Bridge as hereinabove set forth.

Eighth—To enable the said "Brooklyn" to operate said "Local Railroad" and to fulfill the covenants upon its part herein contained, it shall, subject to the reservations herein stated for the uses and purposes mentioned herein, have the full, sole and unobstructed use of the tracks of the "Local Railroad" hereinabove mentioned, together with all switches, sidings, signals, interlocking switches, platforms and stairs connected with such railroad, and all existing appurtenances that are or may be necessary and convenient for the purpose of operating such railroad in the same manner and with the same precautions against accidents as said "Local Railroad" is now operated by said "Commissioner," and also such thereof as may be necessary from time to time, in order to enable said "Brooklyn" to operate the said "Local Railroad" in accordance with such requirements as said "Commissioner" may hereafter give, in order to insure the safe and proper operation of the said Railroad.

Ninth—The "Brooklyn" shall, subject to such reservations as are herein contained, for the purpose of the operation of said "Local Railroad" and the cars or trains of the "Brooklyn" over said Bridge and to enable it to furnish cable power to the "Kings" when said power is required by this contract, or any contract made or to be made with the "Kings" to be used, have the sole and unobstructed use of all the cars, motor cars, cables, cable and electric power plant, storage and switching yards, and all other appurtenances in possession of said "Commissioner" which are used in connection with the operation of the "Local Railroad" over said Bridge, the "Commissioner," however, reserving the right to use so much of said electric plant, and its appurtenances as is or may be required for the lighting of said Bridge and its appurtenances, which lighting and use of said electric power plant for the purpose of said lighting, remains in the exclusive charge and control of said Commissioner, and is not assumed by the "Brooklyn." It being understood and agreed that the "Brooklyn" shall, if required by said "Commissioner," furnish the power and electricity necessary for the lighting of said Bridge and its appurtenances at a cost to be agreed upon by said "Brooklyn" and said "Commissioner," which cost shall be paid by said Commissioner for the power and electricity furnished.

The "Commissioner" reserves the sole control of the shops and of the tools and machinery therein contained. He will keep an account of the work and material which may be used in such shops in doing such maintenance and repairs as the "Brooklyn" is required to do under this contract and the "Brooklyn" shall pay the costs thereof. Such cost shall not, however, exceed the amount which the "Brooklyn" pays for similar work and material. The persons employed in such shops shall be under the exclusive control of said "Commissioner" and shall be employed, paid and discharged in his discretion.

Tenth—This agreement shall not affect the right of the "Kings" to use such of the tracks through the storage yard and across said Bridge as it is authorized by said contract between itself and said Trustees to use in order to permit its trains to pass between its structure in Fulton street in the Borough of Brooklyn and the terminal of said Bridge in Manhattan, nor the right of such Company to use in connection with the "Local Railroad" and the "Brooklyn," the discharging platform and stairs and one-half the space of the loading platform and of the stairs leading to and from the platforms now used by the "Local Railroad" at the Manhattan Borough terminus of the Bridge, as provided in the said contract.

Eleventh—The "Brooklyn" hereby agrees that it will, during the continuance of this agreement, maintain and keep the ties and rails connected with the said "Local Railroad," the rolling stock, electric and cable plants, machinery and all the other property of the "Commissioner" herein mentioned, the custody of which it shall receive under this agreement, in the best of repair and that it will from time to time substitute new ties, new rails, switches and other appurtenances and new tools and machinery in the place of such thereof as may be worn out, and will do and provide everything which may be required to fully maintain and preserve the said "Local Railroad" in the same manner as would be done by the said "Commissioner" if he was operating the same. Such maintenance and repairs shall be subject to the approval of the said "Commissioner" or of his appointee. It shall not be greater than is necessary to preserve the said property in first-class order, reasonable wear and tear considered. Should the "Brooklyn" at any time fail to keep the said railroad and its appurtenances or any part thereof in the best of condition, the Commissioner may give notice in writing to the "Brooklyn" requiring the same to be put in such condition. In case of failure to comply with such notice within sixty days after receipt thereof, he may declare this agreement to be terminated and the operation of the said "Local Railroad" by the "Brooklyn" shall thereupon cease, and the "Brooklyn" will on or before the expiration of said sixty days withdraw its trains, both through and local, from said Bridge and surrender to the "Commissioner" all of the personal property hereinbefore mentioned.

Twelfth—No radical changes are to be made by the "Brooklyn" in either the rolling stock or appurtenances of the said "Local Railroad" without the approval in writing of the "Commissioner."

Thirteenth—The "Brooklyn" may, with the consent of the "Commissioner" discontinue the operation of special trains on the "Local Railroad," always provided that at all hours of the day and night when special trains are not in operation the "Brooklyn" will transport passengers between termini of the Bridge in its through cars at no higher rate of fare than is fixed in the fifth clause hereof relating to fare for passengers using only the "Local Railroad."

PART 2.—FURTHER USE OF THE "LOCAL RAILROAD" TRACKS.

First—For and in consideration of the premises and of the obligations assumed by the "Brooklyn" in the foregoing subdivision of this agreement, and of the payment to be made by the "Brooklyn" to the "Commissioner," of the sum of twenty thousand three hundred and six and 28/100 dollars ($20,306.28) annually, in equal quarterly installments, which the "Brooklyn" agrees to punctually make to said "Commissioner," it is agreed that the "Brooklyn" may, at such times as the tracks reserved for the use of the "Local Railroad" shall not be used by the trains thereof to their full capacity, operate over the same its own trains or cars or the trains or cars of any other railroad with which it may connect and have traffic agreements, to the full capacity of such tracks, provided always, that the cars and also the motive power used in connection with such cars or trains shall be in all respects in conformity with this agreement and with the agreement made between the said Trustees and the "Receiver" of the "Brooklyn" dated August 23, 1897, as hereby modified, and with the proper use of the Bridge, and the same shall as to weight and dimensions of cars and character of motor and of power be subject at all times to the approval of the "Commissioner."

Second—It is understood that the operation of such cars is in no way to affect the amount to be paid for the operation of the " Local Railroad " as hereinabove provided, or the amount which is to be paid as hereinafter provided, in relation to the operation of the cars of the " Brooklyn " over the set of gauntleted tracks reserved for elevated railroads. In other words, so long as the " Brooklyn " pays as toll the amount as hereinafter stated for the operation of its cars over the track reserved for elevated railroads, and upon its part faithfully performs each and all the provisions of this agreement, no additional toll in addition to the said sum of twenty thousand three hundred and six and 28/100 dollars ($20,306.28) is to be charged to it for such cars as it may from time to time operate over the tracks of said " Local Railroad."

Third—It is agreed that the " Brooklyn " will not charge any fare in excess of or in addition to the fare now exacted by it, that is to say, five cents, from any passenger for one continuous ride upon any of its routes in either the Boroughs of Manhattan and Brooklyn, as the case may be, for the carriage of passengers across the said Bridge either over the tracks reserved for said " Local Railroad " or over the tracks reserved for the use of elevated railroads so that the route of said corporation or corporations operated across said Bridge under said contract, so far as the exaction of a fare is concerned, shall be taken and deemed to be a part of the continuous route or one of the continuous routes of the " Brooklyn " or of any railroad with which it may be connected whereon one fare is exacted, so that no additional fare shall be exacted by any elevated railroad corporation from any passenger carried to and from the Bridge and across the Bridge, in addition to the fare exacted from such passenger for carriage to and from the Bridge only.

Fourth—The tracks of the storage yard of the Bridge may be used by the " Brooklyn " for laying up the cars used in operating the " Local Railroad," and such of the cars as it may operate over the same and over the tracks reserved for elevated railroads upon said Bridge.

Part 3.—Modification of Contract of August 23, 1897, as to use of set of Tracks Reserved for Elevated Railroads.

First—The provisions of the aforesaid agreement of August 23, 1897, between the Trustees of the New York and Brooklyn Bridge, and the " Brooklyn," relating to the tolls to be paid by the latter for the operation of its cars over said Bridge, are hereby suspended. In lieu thereof it is agreed that the " Brooklyn " will, during the continuance of this agreement, pay to the " Commissioner " and his successors a toll of ten cents per car for each round trip which a car owned, operated or controlled by the " Brooklyn " shall make over the set of tracks of the Bridge reserved for elevated railroads in and by said contract; and

WHEREAS, it is in contemplation to modify the aforesaid contract between the Trustees of the New York and Brooklyn Bridge and the " Kings," dated August 23, 1897, so that the amount to be paid by it for operating its cars over said Bridge upon said tracks reserved for elevated railroads shall be similar to the amount hereby fixed to be paid by the " Brooklyn " therefor, which is expected to make the receipts of the " Commissioner " from the use of the said tracks by the cars of the said two railroads, not less than the sum of two hundred and fifty dollars ($250) a day; and

WHEREAS, it is expected that the " Kings " will begin to operate its cars over said Bridge on said tracks reserved for elevated railroads, about August 23, 1898, and will thereafter continue such operation, but that until such operation is begun by the " Kings," the " Brooklyn " will be the only elevated road operating over the Bridge: Now, THEREFORE, the " Brooklyn " undertakes and agrees that until the day when the said " Kings " shall begin the operation of its cars across said Bridge, the amount paid by the " Brooklyn " for use of the said tracks upon said Bridge reserved for the elevated railroads granted to it by this agreement shall not be less than the sum of two hundred and fifty dollars ($250) a day, for each and every day from and including the time of the taking effect of this contract, and that it will pay to the said " Commissioner " the sum of two hundred and fifty dollars ($250) per day, and in addition thereto the sum of ten cents (10c.) per round trip, for each car which it shall operate over said set of tracks during that period in excess of twenty-five hundred (2,500) cars a day. From and after the day when the said "Kings" begins the permanent operation of its cars across said Bridge upon said tracks reserved for elevated railroads, and so long as the said cars of said "Kings" are operated over the same, the amount to be paid to the "Commissioner" by the "Brooklyn" under this agreement shall not be less than one hundred and sixty-six and 67/100 dollars ($166.67) a day, together with an additional sum of ten cents (10c.) for each of its cars crossing said Bridge in excess of sixteen hundred and sixty-seven (1,667) cars per day.

In the event that the "Kings" should for any cause discontinue the operation of its cars across said Bridge as a separate and independent corporation at any time during the terms of this contract, then, and in that case, the "Brooklyn" shall resume the payment of a sum equal to two hundred and fifty dollars ($250) per day. Provided that no other elevated railroad corporation is at the time operating cars upon said Bridge; to the end that at no time during the term of this contract shall the income from Elevated Railroad Corporation on said Bridge be less than two hundred and fifty dollars ($250) per day.

Daily reports of the number of cars operated over said set of tracks under this agreement shall be made to the "Commissioner," and the "Brooklyn" shall pay over to him on Monday of each week during the continuance of this agreement the amount hereby required to be paid therefor. Should the "Commissioner" for any cause allow the cars of the "Kings" or any other elevated railroad to be operated over such set of tracks for a less toll than ten cents (10c.) per round trip, then, and in that event, the "Brooklyn" is to pay the same toll as shall be paid by the said other railroad, and the amount of one hundred and sixty-six and 67/100 dollars ($166.67) per day herein guaranteed by the "Brooklyn" as a minimum payment for the use of said set of tracks shall be correspondingly reduced.

In case any other elevated railroad except the "Kings" shall acquire the right to operate its cars or trains over said Bridge and that by reason thereof the "Brooklyn" shall be prevented from operating the full number of sixteen hundred and sixty-seven (1667) cars over said set of tracks, the amount to be guaranteed and paid by it under this paragraph shall be proportionately reduced.

Second—It is further agreed that so much of the provisions of said agreement shall be suspended as provide:

a. That the platform to be constructed by the " Brooklyn " between the tail tracks of said Bridge at the New York (Manhattan Borough) terminal, shall be subject to the control and use of the same by said Trustees, or their successors, and to the use thereof by any subsequent lessee to whom said Trustees may grant the use of the same.

b. That all cars used by the " Brooklyn " on said Bridge shall be subject to inspection by the Bridge authorities and that the latter shall have authority or control over the same in regard to their construction or method of operation while upon said Bridge, and that from the time the trains of the " Brooklyn " enter upon the premises of said Trustees until on the return of the trains from New York they shall depart from said premises, said cars and trains shall be under the management and control of the said Trustees and of their employees.

c. That the Trustees shall have authority to adopt such rules and regulations as to them shall seem reasonable and proper, relating to the transportation of the cars of the " Brooklyn " over said Bridge, including the method of payment of tolls, style of cars, condition of cars, the switching of cars and the use of platforms, to amend and alter any of such rules and regulations and prohibiting the " Brooklyn " from bringing upon the Bridge any cars in which smoking shall be permitted.

d. The provision of paragraph tenth of said agreement, which requires the Trustees to be liable for any delay or accident arising solely from faulty construction or imperfections in the track or appurtenances of the Bridge Railroad.

e. The provision in regard to the number of trains to be delivered by the " Brooklyn " to the said Bridge.

f. The provisions contained in paragraph twelfth of said agreement, providing that the said contract may be terminated by the Trustees before the expiration of ten years from its date.

g. The obligation of the Trustees to furnish men to man the cars of the " Brooklyn."

h. The obligations of the said Trustees to furnish power for the transportation of the cars of the "Brooklyn" over the said Bridge.

Third—In lieu thereof the following provisions are hereby substituted, such substitution to be made with the same force and effect as if they were contained in the said contract when originally executed:

a. The control of the movement of all trains of cars, not hereinbefore provided for upon the said set of tracks reserved for elevated railroads, shall be vested in the "Brooklyn," subject nevertheless to the supervision and authority of the "Commissioner." The "Brooklyn" shall have full and complete power to make and adopt all rules and regulations to be approved of by the "Commissioner" which shall to it seem reasonable and proper relating to the transporting of such cars over said set of tracks, so long as said cars are of proper weight and dimensions, and generally conform to the cars now used by the "Commissioner," and the "Brooklyn" to alter or amend any of such rules or regulations so as to insure the comfort and safety of persons using the cars on said set of tracks on the Bridge, and to subserve the purpose for which said Bridge was constructed. In case, however, objection shall be made by the "Kings" or by any other elevated railroad, which shall hereafter acquire the right to use such set of tracks, to any of such rules, regulations, or to any acts of the "Brooklyn," as being unjust to it, a complaint may be made by it to the "Commissioner," whose decision in regard thereto shall be conclusive and final.

b. The cars of the "Brooklyn" are to be operated over said tracks by its employees.

c. The "Brooklyn" is to furnish at its own expense the power required to operate the cars owned or controlled by it over the said Bridge, and so long as cable power is used for the purpose, it shall furnish such power to the "Kings" and its successor company, at a price to be agreed upon between the said "Brooklyn" and the "Kings." If they cannot agree in regard to such price, the amount thereof shall be determined by the "Commissioner."

d. The "Brooklyn" may, if it elects, and said "Commissioner" approves, discontinue the use of the cable and may in lieu thereof, use electric power only during the hours of the day when the "Local Railroad" is not in operation.

e. The "Brooklyn" shall have the exclusive use of the platform and appurtenances which it has constructed at the Manhattan end of the said Bridge.

f. Said "Brooklyn" shall protect and hold harmless the said "Commissioner" and his successors, and The City of New York, from and against all losses, damages and claims for damage, actions, recoveries, costs, disbursements and expenses of every nature arising from, based upon or connected with, or in any manner charged to be due to any injury to person or property received or sustained by any person upon or in the cars of the "Brooklyn" or the "Local Railroad" whenever and wherever upon the premises of the said "Commissioner" such injuries may arise, be received or sustained, or which may be caused by cars of the said "Brooklyn" or of the "Local Railroad," or which may arise from or be connected with the operation of said cars over said tracks, or in any and every wise growing out of the use of said tracks or any of the premises, appurtenances and appliances thereunto belonging, by the "Brooklyn" or the "Local Railroad." It being also the intention of this agreement that the said "Brooklyn" shall indemnify and hold harmless the said "Commissioner" and his successors for all damages or injury which may be incurred to either person or property by reason of any imperfection in the said tracks covered by this contract or in the appurtenances connected therewith, or of the rolling stock or other property which under the provisions of this agreement are placed under the control of the said "Brooklyn." It being understood, however, that the said "Brooklyn" shall not be liable to the Trustees or to any person, firm or corporation for any damage or hindrance which may arise from faulty construction of any portion of the Bridge not under the control of the said "Brooklyn" or which arises solely from negligence on behalf of the agents or servants of the "Commissioner," or of any other railroad authorized to operate over said Bridge.

Fourth—All the powers reserved to the "Commissioner" and the Chief Engineer of the Bridge mentioned in the agreement of August 23, 1897, relating to supervision, control and management of trains, tracks and appurtenances, platforms, stairs and other matters therein contained, to insure the proper and safe transportation of passengers over the two sets of gauntleted tracks upon said Bridge reserved for elevated railroads, are hereby vested in the " Brooklyn," subject always, however, to the supreme authority of the " Commissioner," as representing The City of New York in the interest of the traveling public, to the end that the operation of the cars of elevated railroad over the railroads of said Bridge shall be under a single head, as aforesaid, so as to insure safety. It being understood that the " Commissioner " will obtain from the " Kings," in a modified agreement to be made between the " Commissioner " and the " Kings," the assent of said company to that effect. In case the " Kings " should not consent to any modification of the agreement of August 23, 1897, and thereby maintain its right to have its trains operated while on the Bridge premises by employees of the " Commissioner," as in said agreement provided, then and in that event the " Brooklyn " agrees to furnish to the " Commissioner " the required number of employees of its own, and charge to him only the amount actually paid to such employees while in charge of trains of the " Kings," which he agrees to pay.

Fifth—The XIII. clause of the agreement of August 23, 1897, is hereby modified to the effect that a new surety bond shall be filed with the " Commissioner " in the amount of two hundred thousand dollars in place of that for fifty thousand dollars heretofore given, which bond shall also secure said " Commissioner," his successors and the said City of New York from all matters relating to the operation of the " Local Railroad " by the " Brooklyn," as provided in part One of this agreement, as also of the cars authorized to be operated under parts Two and Three thereof. The " Commissioner " agrees, however, that he will hold the surety bond of the " Kings " or any renewal thereof as security to indemnify the " Brooklyn," if it should be determined that any damage done to the Bridge or to persons or property was caused by the negligence of the " Kings " or of its employees.

Sixth—Should the " Brooklyn " fail to make promptly any of the payments herein reserved, or otherwise violate any of the stipulations and provisions of this agreement, then the " Commissioner " may, on sixty (60) days written notice, declare this agreement terminated, and after the expiration of said sixty (60) days the "Brooklyn" shall forfeit all rights and privileges under this agreement. Said "Commissioner" may also hold the "Brooklyn" and its surety liable for any and all damages which the said "Commissioner" had to that time sustained because of the default of the "Brooklyn."

Seventh—Notwithstanding the modifications and substitutions of the various clauses of the agreement of August 23, 1897, as herein provided, nothing herein contained shall have the effect of abrogating said agreement. The intention being that such of its provisions as are inconsistent with this agreement are suspended while this agreement is in force. Should, for any reason, this agreement terminate before the time herein stated, then and in that event the agreement of August 23, 1897, shall still be valid in all respects and of the same force and effect as if this agreement had not been executed, except that a violation of any of the terms and conditions of this agreement may be deemed a violation of the agreement of August 23, 1897, and may subject the "Brooklyn" to a forfeiture of that contract and this contract, in the discretion of the "Commissioner," upon such notice of forfeiture as is provided herein.

Eighth—The execution of this agreement by the "Receiver" is contingent upon his obtaining an order of court approving of the same, and the same is not to take effect until such an order has been made.

Ninth—This agreement shall terminate at the time and upon the conditions stated in the said contract between the said Trustees and the "Brooklyn," dated August 23, 1897, thereof.

Tenth—In case the Bridge is totally destroyed by fire, the elements, or otherwise, this agreement shall terminate and the "Commissioner" shall be under no obligation to restore the same. In case the same shall be restored, the "Brooklyn" shall have the option to reinstate said agreement for the unexpired term thereof.

If the destruction shall be partial, this agreement shall be suspended until the Bridge and its appurtenances shall have been restored.

If any injury shall be done to the railroad, rolling stock or appurtenances of the Bridge by collision of cars or otherwise by negligence of the "Brooklyn," it shall forthwith restore the same or pay the value thereof to the "Commissioner."

Eleventh—The rolling stock and appurtenances connected with said Bridge and covered by this agreement are to be kept insured by the "Commissioner." In case of their destruction or injury by fire the amount collected upon the policies covering the same is to be expended in replacing or repairing the same.

IN WITNESS WHEREOF, the said "Commissioner" and "Receiver" have hereunto set their respective hands and seals, and the "Brooklyn" has caused its corporate seal to be hereto affixed, and this instrument to be subscribed by its President and Assistant and Acting Secretary, the day and year first above written.

JOHN L. SHEA, [SEAL.]
Commissioner of Bridges, City of New York.

FRED. UHLMANN, [SEAL.]
Receiver.

BROOKLYN ELEVATED RAILROAD COMPANY,
[SEAL.] By FRED. UHLMANN,
President.

Attest:
JOHN W. W. MITCHELL,
Assistant Secretary.

STATE OF NEW YORK, } ss.:
County of New York,

On this 24th day of June, in the year one thousand eight hundred and ninety-eight, before me personally came John L. Shea, to me known and known to me to be the Commissioner of Bridges of The City of New York and to be the person named in and who executed the foregoing instrument as "Commissioner," and he acknowledged to me that he executed the same as such "Commissioner."

W. H. BRADY,
[SEAL.] Notary Public,
N. Y. County.

STATE OF NEW YORK, } ss.:
County of New York,

On this 24th day of June, in the year one thousand eight hundred and ninety-eight, before me personally came Frederick Uhlmann, to me known and known to me to be the Receiver of the Brooklyn Elevated Railroad Company and of the Union Elevated Railroad Company, and to be the preson named in and who executed the foregoing instrument as such Receiver, and he acknowledged to me that he executed the same as such Receiver.

W. H. BRADY,
[SEAL.] Notary Public,
N. Y. County.

STATE OF NEW YORK, } ss.:
County of New York,

On this 24th day of June, in the year one thousand eight hundred and ninety-eight, before me personally came Frederick Uhlmann and John W. W. Mitchell, with whom I am personally acquainted, who being by me duly sworn, each for himself deposes and says: The said Frederick Uhlmann that he resides in the Borough of Manhattan, City of New York; that at the time of the execution of the foregoing instrument he was the President of the Brooklyn Elevated Railroad Company; the said John W. W. Mitchell, that he resided in the Borough of Brooklyn, City of New York, and at the time of the execution of the foregoing instrument he was the Assistant and Acting Secretary of the Brooklyn Elevated Railroad Company; that each knew the corporate seal of said Brooklyn Elevated Railroad Company; that the seal affixed to such foregoing instrument was such corporate seal, and that it was affixed by order of the Board of Directors of said Company, and that each signed his name thereto by a like order respectively as President and Assistant and Acting Secretary of said Company.

W. H. BRADY,
[SEAL.] Notary Public,
N. Y. County.

AGREEMENTS.

THE BROOKLYN HEIGHTS RAILROAD COMPANY, NEW YORK CITY RAILWAY COMPANY,

THE CONEY ISLAND AND BROOKLYN RAILROAD COMPANY,

BRIDGE OPERATING COMPANY.

FOR OPERATION OF SURFACE CARS ON WILLIAMSBURG BRIDGE.

DATED MAY 21, 1904.

AGREEMENT, made this twenty-first day of May, 1904, by and between THE CITY OF NEW YORK (hereinafter called the "CITY"), party of the first part, by the COMMISSIONER OF BRIDGES (hereinafter called the "COMMISSIONER"); THE BROOKLYN HEIGHTS RAILROAD COMPANY (hereinafter called the "BROOKLYN COMPANY"), party of the second part; THE CONEY ISLAND AND BROOKLYN RAILROAD COMPANY (hereinafter called the "CONEY ISLAND COMPANY"), party of the third part; THE NEW YORK CITY RAILWAY COMPANY (hereinafter called the "NEW YORK COMPANY"), party of the fourth part; and the BRIDGE OPERATING COMPANY (hereinafter called the "BRIDGE COMPANY"), party of the fifth part.

WHEREAS, the "City" is the owner of the bridge and approaches thereto, substantially, but not yet entirely, completed, across the East river, known as the Williamsburg Bridge, which, together with all approaches and appurtenances thereto, is hereinafter called the Bridge; and,

WHEREAS, the "City" is now engaged in the completion of the Bridge, including the construction of four sets of railway tracks for surface cars across the Bridge, with loops and switches, sidings, platforms, stations and other structures and appurtenances necessary in operating trolley cars upon the respective terminals of the Bridge and across the Bridge, substantially in accordance with the plans and specifications hereto annexed marked " Exhibit A," all of such construction work thus indicated in " Exhibit A " being hereinafter designated the surface tracks; and in the construction of the necessary apparatus, conveniences and appliances for the operation by electricity as a motive power of the north pair of surface tracks by the underground electric system, and of the south pair of surface tracks by the overhead trolley system, substantially in accordance with the plans and specifications hereto annexed marked " Exhibit B," all of such apparatus, conveniences and appliances thus indicated in " Exhibit B," including all construction, special or otherwise, required to equip the northerly pair of tracks for operation by the underground electric system, as well as all construction required to equip the southerly pair of tracks for operation by the overhead electric system, being hereinafter called electrical equipment of the surface tracks; all of the surface tracks and electrical equipment thereof to constitute a part of the Bridge and to be the property of the City, so that the operation of the Bridge may be more effective, and the transportation facilities afforded by the Bridge may be enlarged, by the operation of cars on the surface tracks forming a part of the Bridge as aforesaid; and,

WHEREAS, the " Commissioner " has determined it to be in the public interest that the " City " shall contract with corporations to operate cars on the surface tracks with the electrical equipment thereof; and,

WHEREAS, the " Brooklyn Company," the " Coney Island Company," the " New York Company " and the " Bridge Company " have entered, or are about to enter, into a contract in writing with each other, bearing even date herewith, in relation to the operation of cars upon that portion of the Bridge consisting of the surface tracks and the electrical equipment thereof;

Now, THEREFORE, in consideration of the mutual covenants herein contained, THIS AGREEMENT WITNESSETH:

I.—The "City" agrees to complete as soon as practicable the Bridge, and particularly that portion thereof consisting of the surface tracks and the electrical equipment thereof, substantially in accordance with the plans and specifications hereto annexed marked "Exhibit A" and "Exhibit B," respectively, the surface tracks and the electrical equipment thereof so to be completed by the City to be and constitute a part of the Bridge and to be the property of the City.

II.—The "Bridge Company" shall pay to the "City" for the use of the aforesaid electrical equipment, the loops and other terminal facilities, located within the limits of the Bridge property, pending the existence of this contract, a rental of ten thousand dollars per annum, payable quarterly.

III.—The "City" agrees that as soon as that portion of the Bridge consisting of the surface tracks and the electrical equipment thereof shall be completed and ready for operation, then the cars on the surface tracks with the electrical equipment thereof shall be operated thereafter, until ten years from September 1, 1904, by the "Bridge Company," the "Brooklyn Company," the "Coney Island Company" and the "New York Company," as hereinafter provided. After the termination of said period, operation of cars upon the surface tracks shall be continued by the said four companies under the terms and conditions of this contract until one year after the "Commissioner" shall have notified said companies to cease such operation, but after the expiration of said period either of said four companies shall have the right to cease operation, provided it shall have given the "Commissioner" one year's notice of its intention so to do.

IV.—The "Bridge Company" agrees that as soon as that portion of the Bridge consisting of the surface tracks and the electrical equipment thereof shall be completed and ready for the operation of cars thereon, then the "Bridge Company" will furnish and supply, for the operation thereof during the term of this contract, a sufficient number of cars, suitably equipped for operation with electricity as a motive power by both the overhead and the underground trolley systems, and electricity proper and sufficient for such operation, so that such cars may be operated either on the north pair of surface tracks or the south pair of surface tracks; and the "Bridge Company" agrees thereupon to commence, and thereafter during the term of this contract to continue, the operation of such cars on said surface tracks, by electricity as a motive power, back and forth over said surface tracks, of a sufficient number and with such frequency as to reasonably accommodate the traveling public. The character and equipment of the cars so furnished, the number thereof and the frequency and mode of operation shall be such as the "Commissioner" shall approve and direct.

The "City" agrees as soon as practicable and about July 15, 1904, to complete the south pair of surface tracks with the electrical equipment pertaining thereto and including two loops connecting therewith on the Brooklyn Plaza, and the "Bridge Company" agrees that it will by the same date complete a temporary stub terminal connecting with these tracks and on a line therewith on the ground east of Clinton street in Manhattan.

The "Bridge Company" agrees that as soon as these tracks, loops, this stub terminal and the electrical equipment pertaining thereto, are completed, that it will operate this portion of the surface tracks and electrical equipment as the "Commissioner" may direct, until the full completion of the surface tracks and electric equipment, and on the same terms and conditions of this contract, and at the same rate of toll per car and at the rate of fare for local service, but the annual rental shall not begin until the full completion of the surface tracks and electrical equipment.

The "Commissioner" shall have the right to change the number and location of any of the loops, switches and tracks on the Bridge property at its terminals, in any manner which shall seem to him proper to facilitate the movement of passengers from or to the railway cars crossing the Bridge, but such changes shall only be made after full consultation with the second, third and fourth parties to this agreement.

V.—The "Bridge Company" agrees to keep and maintain the surface tracks and the electrical equipment thereof in good order and repair, and in such manner as the "Commissioner" may approve or direct, during the term of this contract.

VI.—The "Bridge Company" shall be entitled to charge a rate of fare of three cents, or less, for a single ticket or a single fare, entitling each person, actually or apparently more than three years old, to one passage across the Bridge between the terminals of the surface tracks, and shall keep on sale, in such manner as shall be approved or directed by the "Commissioner." tickets at the rate of two tickets for five cents, each of which tickets shall entitle any person actually or apparently over three years of age to one passage across the Bridge between the terminals of the surface tracks; and the "Bridge Company" shall carry every person actually and apparently under three years of age, free, when attended by a person over ten years of age.

VII.—The "New York Company" agrees that as soon as that portion of the Bridge consisting of the north pair of surface tracks and the electrical equipment thereof shall be completed and ready for operation, then the "New York Company" will commence and continue during the term of this contract the operation of cars over said north pair of surface tracks, in connection with the street surface railroad operated by it in the Borough of Manhattan which shall then be connected with the said surface tracks, as hereinafter provided.

VIII.—The "Brooklyn Company" and the "Coney Island Company" agree that as soon as that portion of the Bridge consisting of the south pair of surface tracks and the electrical equipment thereof shall be completed and ready for operation, then the "Brooklyn Company" and the "Coney Island Company" will commence and continue during the term of this contract the operation of cars over the said south pair of surface tracks, in connection with the street surface railroads operated by them, respectively, in the Borough of Brooklyn, which shall then be connected with the trolley tracks, as hereinafter provided.

IX.—The "Brooklyn Company," the "Coney Island Company" and the "New York Company" agree that in their operation of the surface tracks with the electrical equipment thereof, they will not unnecessarily interfere with the operation thereof by the "Bridge Company" as approved and directed by the "Commissioner."

X.—The "City" imposes and will exact the sum of five cents per round trip for each and every car operated or transported by each of said four companies, respectively, across the Bridge, and by each Company admitted upon said Bridge by either party hereto. Such payment shall be made to the "Commissioner" by each of said companies, respectively, from time to time, at such intervals as the "Commissioner" shall determine.

XI.—The "City" hereby agrees that the "Brooklyn Company" may connect the street surface railroad in the Borough of Brooklyn operated by the "Brooklyn Company" and next adjoining the surface tracks, with the south pair of surface tracks, substantially as indicated by the plans and specifications hereto annexed, marked "Exhibit A" and "Exhibit B," and the "Brooklyn Company" agrees to make such connections as soon as practicable. No fare in addition to the fare charged and paid for transportation over the surface railroads of said companies, respectively, shall be charged by the "Brooklyn Company" or the "Coney Island Company" to through passengers for transportation across the Bridge on the cars of their respective lines; but the "Brooklyn Company" and the "Coney Island Company" may charge each passenger actually or apparently over three years of age, transported on their respective cars across the Bridge, a fare of five cents for such transportation, but shall carry each such passenger actually and apparently under three years of age across the Bridge free, if attended by a person over ten years of age.

XII.—The "City" hereby agrees that the "New York Company" may connect the street surface railroad in the Borough of Manhattan operated by the "New York Company" and next adjoining the surface tracks, with the north pair of surface tracks, substantially as indicated by the plans and specifications hereto annexed marked "Exhibit A" and "Exhibit B," and the "New York Company" agrees to make such connection as soon as practicable. No fare in addition to the fare charged and paid for transportation over the surface railroads of said Company shall be charged by the "New York Company" to through passengers for transportation across the Bridge on its cars; but the "New York Company" may charge each passenger actually or apparently over three years of age, transported on its cars across the Bridge a fare of five cents for such transportation, but shall carry each such passenger actually and apparently under three years of age across the Bridge free, if attended by a person over ten years of age.

XIII.—The "New York Company" may, with the approval of the "Commissioner," permit any other company operating a street surface railroad in the Borough of Manhattan to operate its cars over the northerly pair of surface tracks; and the "Brooklyn Company" and the "Coney Island Company," respectively, may, with the approval of the "Commissioner," permit any other company operating a street surface railroad in the Borough of Brooklyn to operate its cars over the southerly pair of tracks; but operation across the Bridge by any such additional company shall in all respects be subject to all the terms and conditions of this contract as fully as if such additional company were a party hereto; and the total number of through cars operated across the Bridge by the "Brooklyn Company" and all companies admitted to the Bridge by it shall not in any one hour exceed eighty-four per cent. (84%) of the through cars operated across the Bridge upon the southerly pair of tracks during such hour, nor shall the total number of through cars operated across the Bridge by the "Coney Island Company" and all companies admitted to the Bridge by it exceed in any one hour sixteen per cent. (16%) of the through cars operated across the Bridge upon the southerly pair of tracks during such hour.

XIV.—The "Bridge Company," the "Brooklyn Company," the "Coney Island Company," and the "New York Company," jointly and severally agree to protect and hold harmless the "City" and the "Commissioner" from and against all losses, damages and claims for damages, actions, recoveries, costs, disbursements and expenses of every nature arising from, based upon, connected with or in any manner chargeable to injury to person or property, received or sustained by any person upon or in the cars operated by either of the said four companies, whenever and wherever upon the Bridge such injuries may arise, be received or sustained, or which may be caused by the cars of either of the said four companies, or which may arise from or be connected with the presence and operation of such cars upon the Bridge, or which shall in any wise be connected with or arise out of the bringing of the said cars upon the Bridge, or transporting or operating them upon, over or across the Bridge, or in any and every wise growing out of the use of the Bridge by either of the said four companies; and further to protect and hold harmless the "City" and the "Commissioner" from and against losses, damages and claims for damages, actions, recoveries, costs, disbursements and expenses of every nature which may arise or result from any failure or delay on the part of either of the said four companies to promptly and regularly operate and transport cars across the Bridge in either direction, or for any delay or hindrance to said cars while in tansit from whatever cause or reason such neglect or refusal or delay may arise, or which may arise to any person using the Bridge in any way or manner, who shall be injured in person or property, or hindered or delayed in the use of the Bridge by reason of any matter, thing or occurrence arising from or connected with the operation of said cars across or upon the Bridge. Provided, however, that the foregoing provisions shall not include indemnity against any such losses, damages, claims, failure, injuries, hindrances or delays caused by public disturbances, acts of God, inevitable accident, or any defect in, or accident to, that portion of the Bridge over which the said aforesaid companies have no control.

XV.—The "Commissioner" shall have full and complete power to make and adopt rules and regulations relating to the operation of cars over the Bridge, including the method of ascertaining the amount of payments hereinbefore provided to be made, the number of cars, the rate of speed of said cars, the movement and headway thereof, the style of cars to be used and the condition thereof, the switching of cars and the use of platforms, and regulations for governing and controlling the electrical current for operating said cars upon and across the Bridge, and to amend or alter any such rules and regulations so as to secure the safety and comfort of persons using the

Bridge and to subserve the purposes for which the Bridge was constructed. But each of the said four companies shall have reasonable notice of such rules and regulations and of the amendments or alterations thereof.

XVI.—All cars used on the Bridge by any of the said four companies and all equipment and appliances relating thereto, located on the Bridge, shall be subject at all times to inspection by the "Commissioner" or his authorized representative, who shall have power to forbid rights on the Bridge to cars that may for any reason be unsatisfactory, and to direct the removal of any old or inadequate appliances, and to substitute therefor others of approved character; and the said supervision, management and control of said cars shall in every particular and at all times be wholly exercised by the "Commissioner" from the entering of said cars upon the Bridge to the departure of said cars from the Bridge, and the said "Commissioner" shall at all times regulate and limit in his discretion the total number of cars which may be operated upon the said north pair of surface tracks and the total number of cars which may be operated upon the said south pair of surface tracks and the total number of cars which shall be operated by the "Bridge Company."

All employees of each of the said four companies, motormen, conductors, inspectors and others employed in connection with the operation of the said cars upon and over the Bridge and in connection with the operation thereof upon the Bridge, shall be of good character and skilled in their occupation.

XVII.—The "Bridge Company" having not yet been incorporated, the "New York Company," the "Brooklyn Company" and the "Coney Island Company" agree that they will procure the incorporation of the "Bridge Company" and the execution by it of this contract before the completion of either pair of surface tracks.

XVIII.—This contract shall be binding upon and inure to the benefit of the successors and assigns of the respective parties hereto.

IN WITNESS WHEREOF, the "City" has caused its corporate name to be hereunto signed by the "Commissioner" and its corporate seal to be hereto duly affixed, and each of the other parties hereto has caused its corporate name to be hereunto signed and its corporate seal to be hereto affixed by its officers thereunto duly authorized, the day and year first above written:

The City of New York,

By George E. Best,
Commissioner of Bridges.

The New York City Railway Company,
By H. H. Vreeland,
President.

[L. S.]
Attest:
    Charles E. Warren,
        Secretary.

The Coney Island and Brooklyn Railroad Company,

By John L. Heins,
President.

[L. S.]
Attest:
    Duncan B. Cannon,
        Secretary.

The Brooklyn Heights Railroad Company,

By E. W. Winter,
President.

[L. S.]
Attest:
    C. D. Meneely,
        Secretary.

Bridge Operating Company,

By E. W. Winter,
President.

[L. S.]
Attest:
    C. D. Meneely,
        Secretary.

STATE OF NEW YORK, } ss.:
County of New York,

On this 21st day of May, 1904, before me personally appeared George E. Best, to me known and known to me to be one of the individuals described in and who executed the foregoing instrument, and he acknowledged to me that he executed the same as Commissioner of Bridges of The City of New York.

FREDERICK GOLDSMITH,
Commissioner of Deeds,
N. Y. City.

STATE OF NEW YORK, } ss.:
County of New York,

On this 21st day of May, 1904, before me personally appeared H. H. Vreeland, John L. Heins, E. W. Winter, Charles E. Warren, Duncan B. Cannon and C. D. Meneely, to me severally known to be the persons who executed the foregoing instrument as President of the New York City Railway Company, President of the Coney Island and Brooklyn Railroad Company, President of The Brooklyn Heights Railroad Company, Secretary of the New York City Railway Company, Secretary of the Coney Island and Brooklyn Railroad Company, and Secretary of The Brooklyn Heights Railroad Company, respectively, who, being by me duly and severally sworn did each depose and say the said H. H. Vreeland and the said Charles E. Warren that he was President and Secretary, respectively, of the New York City Railroad Company and knows the corporate seal thereof; the said John L. Heins and Duncan B. Cannon, that he was the President and Secretary, respectively, of the Coney Island and Brooklyn Railroad Company and knows the corporate seal thereof; and the said E. W. Winter and C. D. Meneely, that he was the President and Secretary, respectively, of The Brooklyn Heights Railroad Company and knows the corporate seal thereof; the said Vreeland and Warren did each say that the seal of the New York City Railway Company thereto affixed was the corporate seal of said Company; and the said John L. Heins and Duncan B. Cannon did each say that the seal of the Coney Island and Brooklyn Railroad Company thereto affixed was the corporate seal of said company; and the said E. W. Winter and C. D. Meneely did each say that the seal of The Brooklyn Heights Railroad Company thereto affixed was the corporate seal of said Company; and each of said persons did further say that the corporate seal of the Company of which he was an officer as aforesaid, was so affixed by order of the Board of Directors of his respective Company, and that he signed his name thereto as President or Secretary, respectively, by the like order.

IN WITNESS WHEREOF, I have hereunto set my hand and seal the day and year above set forth.

FREDERICK GOLDSMITH,
Commissioner of Deeds,
N. Y. City.

STATE OF NEW YORK, } ss.:
County of Kings,

On this 6th day of September, 1904, personally before me appeared E. W. Winter and C. D. Meneely, to me known, who being by me duly sworn, did each for himself depose and say: the said E. W. Winter that he resided in the Borough of Manhattan, City of New York, and is President of Bridge Operating Company, the said C. D. Meneely that he resides in the Borough of Brooklyn, City of New York, and is the Secretary of Bridge Operating Company, the corporation described in and which executed the within instrument, that he knew the seal of said corporation, that the seal affixed to said instrument was such corporate seal, that it was affixed thereto by order of the Board of Directors, and that he signed his name thereto by like order.

[SEAL.] D. F. URQUHART, JR.,
Notary Public,
Kings County, N. Y.

Oversized Foldout

Oversized Foldout

Oversized Foldout

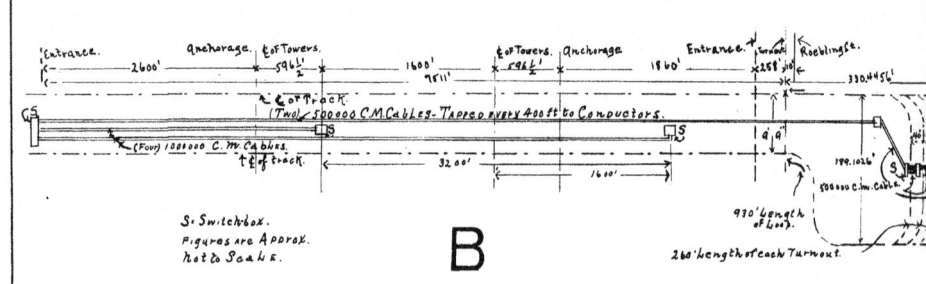

Date Due

Transportation
Library

TG
25
.N5
A42
1906

N.Y.(City) Dept. of
   Bridges.
   Contracts with
r.r. companies